# Vessel

A MEMOIR

## Cai Chongda

Translated from the Chinese
by Dylan Levi King

HARPERVIA

*An Imprint of* HarperCollins*Publishers*

HarperCollins books may be purchased for educational, business, or sales promotional use. For information, please email the Special Markets Department at SPsales@harpercollins.com.

Originally published as *Pinang* in China in 2014 by Guomai Culture and Media Co. Ltd.

FIRST HARPERVIA HARDCOVER PUBLISHED IN 2021

Library of Congress Cataloging-in-Publication Data

Names: Cai, Chongda, 1982- author. | King, Dylan Levi, translator.
Title: Vessel: a memoir / Chongda Cai; translated from the Chinese by Dylan Levi King.
Other titles: Pi nang. English
Description: First HarperVia hardcover edition. | New York: HarperVia, 2021. | "Originally published as Pinang in China in 2014 by Guomai Culture and Media Co. Ltd."
Identifiers: LCCN 2020051051 | ISBN 9780063038004 (hardcover) | ISBN 9780063038011 (paperback) | ISBN 9780063038028 (ebook)
Subjects: LCSH: Cai, Chongda, 1982- | Cai, Chongda, 1982—Family. | Fujian Sheng (China)—Social life and customs—20th century. | Working class families—China—Fujian Sheng. | Dongshi (China)—Biography.
Classification: LCC DS793.F8 C3413 2021 | DDC 951.24/5 [B]—dc23
LC record available at https://lccn.loc.gov/2020051051

21 22 23 24 25   LSC   10 9 8 7 6 5 4 3 2 1

# Contents

# Vessel

Nana, my great-grandmother on my mother's side, lived to the age of ninety-nine. She was a tough woman. Her daughter, my grandmother, passed away in her fifties. Parents should never have to bury their children, but that's exactly what my nana had to do. The relatives worried about how she would take it, so they took turns watching over her. As the time to see her daughter off came, she became angry. For reasons that were unclear even to her, she stalked the house, cursing to herself. She opened the lid of the coffin to look at her daughter, then went to the kitchen to inspect the offerings for the funeral. When she went back into the main room, she saw someone trying to kill a chicken. They had cut the neck of the bird but hadn't managed to sever its carotid artery. The chicken was running around, dripping blood everywhere. She ran over, grabbed the chicken, and flung it to the floor furiously.

The feet of the chicken clawed at thin air, then finally

stopped moving. "You have to finish it—don't let the body torture the soul." She wasn't an educated woman, but she had a reputation as a sort of witch doctor. She occasionally came out with a phrase that seemed to have been pulled from a dusty tome.

Everyone was struck dumb.

She didn't cry at the funeral. Even when my grandmother's body was being put into the crematory, she only cast a sidelong glance at the scene, as if expressing silent disdain for those who wept and wailed—or perhaps she was simply an old woman drowsing.

I was just going into first grade that year. I didn't understand how she could be so cold-blooded. During the funeral, I went over to her side a few times to ask her, "Nana, how come you're not sad?" Her liver-spotted face smoothed and softened. That was Nana's smile.

"It is because I hold no grudges," she said.

It was something I heard her say many times later in life. After my grandmother died, she often came to stay with us. She said, "Before your grandmother died, she told me, Blackie doesn't have a grandpa or grandma, and his parents are always busy. I want you to look after him."

Nana was a ruthless woman. You could see it even in the way she chopped vegetables. She chopped down on the stems and leaves with the same force she used to whack through spareribs. One time she was working in the kitchen, and I heard a very calm "ai-ya."

I shouted back, "What's wrong, Nana?"

"I'm fine," she said. "I just cut the tip of my finger off." Everyone in the family started rushing around, but through it all she remained stone-faced.

My mother and I sat on a bench in the hospital hallway while she was having her fingertip sutured back on. My mother told me a story about her. When Nana's son—my mother's uncle—was still young and hadn't yet learned how to swim, she threw him in the ocean. That was her way of teaching him to swim. He came close to drowning, but a neighbor was nearby and ended up jumping in to save him. A few days later, the same neighbor saw her throw her son into the ocean again. When she heard people calling her cold-hearted, she coldly replied, "Make your body serve you, not the other way around!"

When she got out of the hospital, I asked her if the story was true. I couldn't help myself. "It's true," she said flatly. "Your body's a vessel. If you wait on it to do something, there's no hope for you. If you put your body to work, you can start to live." To be honest, at the time I didn't understand.

I always thought she must have been carved from stone: she was so hard that nothing could hurt her. In our small town, she had a reputation as a tough old woman. Even in her nineties, she would totter on her bound feet by herself from her village to the town. When we tried to get her a car to go back, she would always erupt: "You've got two choices, you either walk with me or I walk back by myself." So it became a frequent scene on the flagstone path that led to the edge of town: a young man supporting the old woman as she walked back home.

But as strong as she was, I did see her cry. This happened when she was around ninety-two years old. She had climbed up on her roof to fix a hole. She was careless, lost her footing, and slipped off. When she came inside, she could only lie motionless on her bed. I went to visit her. She heard me coming, and before I even opened the door, she cried out, "My great-grandson, such a good boy. . . . Your nana can't move. Nana is stuck here." A week later she stubbornly insisted on getting back on her feet, but she only managed a few steps before she fell again. She cried and made me promise that I would come see her as often as I could. She got up every day and leaned on a chair to make her way to the front door. She sat there waiting for me. I went to visit as often as I could, and even after she had recovered, I kept going, especially when something was bothering me. Sitting with her, I felt an indescribable peacefulness.

I started to see her less frequently after I went to university and then took a job in another city. But whenever I was going through difficult times, I asked for leave and went back to sit with her for an afternoon. When I told her what was troubling me, she didn't always understand—she was hard of hearing, too, so maybe she didn't even hear me. Whenever I saw a slightly perplexed smile spread across her face, smoothing the wrinkles that the years had carved, I felt completely at ease.

I found out about her passing on a completely ordinary morning. My mother called to tell me that she was gone, and then both of us began to cry. She told me that Nana had wanted to tell me this: "Don't let Blackie cry. Death is just another rung on the ladder. If you remember me, I will be there. It'll be even easier to come visit you now that I'm free of this body."

It was only then that I finally understood what she had said to me, that I understood her outlook on life: life would be easy if we weren't dragged down by the body and all its base desires. Nana, I remember. "If you wait around all day for this vessel, there's no hope for you. If you can put your body to some use, you can start to live." Please promise you will come to see me.

# 2

# My Mother's House

My mother wanted to build the house even though she knew very well that it might stand for a year or less before it was torn down.

She was on her way back from the municipal government offices when she decided. She had seen the demolition plans on one of the walls in an exhibition room. The pencil line on the map had been hastily scrawled, but it was clear enough that it cleaved through our piece of land like a knife splitting a block of tofu.

She thought she could even hear the sound of the line splitting her new house—not an abrupt crack but a resounding gong. The sound echoed in her ears the whole way back. She told me she had a headache.

"Maybe it's this weather," she said. "No fresh air. Maybe I'm just tired from the walk. Maybe it's this dry winter." She asked me if we could rest. She leaned against the wall of a house along the road. She turned away from me and covered her face with her hand.

I knew it had nothing to do with the weather. I knew it had nothing to do with her being tired. I knew it wasn't because the winter air was too dry. I knew that what she was trying to do with her face buried against the wall was to calm the rough seas of her own heart.

The four-story house we were going home to wasn't much to look at. Even without going inside, you would know it was no palace. The lot it sat on was about two thousand square feet, with the big house on the north half, sitting in a messy yard—an older brick house, its facade mottled by age. It would be obvious to anyone looking at it that the four-story house had not been put up all at once: the two lower floors were facing west, with two big doors opening on the road, part of a naive scheme of my mother's to run a shop there; the two upper floors faced south, and they seemed unfinished, displaying exposed brick and concrete.

Every time I came home from Beijing, as I walked down the small alley toward the yard and saw the house in the distance, I always thought of coral. That is how coral grows—rising upward and then, when it dies, providing a home for other coral, which keeps rising upward. The circle of life keeps turning, and the dead and the living are piled up together.

Sometimes when I was at my desk and got tired of working, I brought up my hometown on Google Maps, slowly zooming in, closer and closer, until I could see the rough outline of my home. I could go from the pale blue globe of Earth and focus downward to the house nestled awkwardly on our land. But I thought of all the people who must have seen the houses over the years, whether walking down that alley or even looking idly out of an airplane window: they wouldn't have even noticed it, let alone taken a second look. Who would even guess at the heart-rending stories I could tell you about what has happened within those walls? Once again, it's like coral, the pieces of coral nestled at the bottom of an aquarium. Their purpose is to enhance by contrast the beauty of the fish in the tank. The life cycle of coral, with its story of death and inheritance, might be just as moving as my own story, but who is going to pay it any mind?

I've heard the story of this plot of land many times. My mother was twenty-four, and my father was twenty-seven. Their first meeting was supervised by a matchmaker. They were too shy to look each other in the eye, and the future courses of their lives were intertwined in that moment. The government had confiscated the land of my father's father, and any ambitions he had were replaced by an opium pipe. By the time my father was in his teens, he knew none of the family's sons would have any help finding a wife. He had no house and no money. On my parents' first date, my father took my mother to that piece of land and promised he would buy it for her and build a big house on it.

My mother believed him.

They bought the land three years after being married. My father took the money he had saved and combined it with the paltry sum he had received as a dowry from my mother's family. After that came the problem of coming up with the money to build the house. But my father was still mixed up in a gang at the time, and he was fearless. He pounded his chest and stormed off to get the money. He decided to build at the front of the property, leaving room for another wing, which he said he would build later.

My father never went back on his word. My mother always remembers that as his most glorious moment.

She recalled how she worried about their debt—the thousands they owed and the look on my father's face when he told her, "It'll be easy to pay back!" She talked about that time with emotion, and she always ended by saying that at that moment, she knew our father was a real man.

But my father turned out not to be quite as brave as he imagined. The only reason he had been so fearless was because he had no idea how much there was to fear. That was something my mother often said in later years to mock him.

The year after that, my father had his son. That is where I enter the story. Family legend has it that he suffered terrible insomnia the night after he held his tiny son in his arms. The next morning he got up at six or seven and shook my mother awake, saying, "What the hell is wrong with me?"

The fearless, carefree man was replaced by the frowning, worried father I came to know. Anxiety chipped away at his appetite. My mother had already realized that he was not as invincible as he had seemed. Three days after I was born, my mother and I were discharged. My parents had no money to pay for a longer stay.

I was actually my parents' second child. My sister came first. Worry hung over their heads that my father would be fired from his state job for violating the one-child policy. That was the reason they had gone to Xiamen for my birth. The only way to get home was to hitchhike. My father carried me, while my mother, weak from the birth, tried her best to look after herself. Without saying a word, they walked together to the highway. They weren't really even sure how to get home.

They came to a lake. My father stopped beside the lake and looked out at it, squinting. He turned to my mother and said, "Can we really make it home?"

My mother was in so much pain that every step felt like her last, but she forced a smile and said, "Just a few more steps. God always provides a path."

My father took a few steps and turned around. "Can we really make it home?"

He took a few more steps.

He kept going until he came to an intersection. The driver of the next car to stop was someone from our hometown on his way back after a trip to Xiamen to resupply his shop.

"Just a few more steps." Because it had been successful the first time, my mother never stopped saying it. She had staked her future on my father, and that was how she encouraged him.

As he had feared, my father was fired from his state job and fined three years of grain rations. Weak with anxiety, he was paralyzed by the news. He refused to look for work. My mother kept silent. She looked for jobs herself and made what she could, sewing clothes, weaving, stuffing things. My mother stole the charcoal my family burned from the neighbors. She begged for the fish we ate for dinner from relatives. She didn't comfort my father, and she didn't lose her temper. For three years, she quietly went about the work of supporting our household. Things changed on one fateful day when my father took his usual stroll to the front gate. He stood beside the gate and looked at the vegetables my mother was growing and the ducks and chickens she had raised. He turned around and went back inside to tell my mother, "I'm going to find a job." A month later, he went to Ningbo to work as a sailor.

Three years later, my father returned with enough money to build a brick house.

My father spent a bundle. He hired a stonemason to carve a stone tablet for the gate featuring a pair of birds and a poetic couplet composed with his and my mother's names. My father had the mason work in secret and asked him to wrap it in red cloth after it was put up on the gate. When the time came, my father revealed it by tearing away the cloth. That was how their two names came to grace the first brick house.

I was six years old at the time. I saw my mother staring at the couplet, speechless, her hand covering her mouth. A few steps away, my father looked on proudly.

The next day, a banquet was held to celebrate. My father made another announcement: he was not going back to work in Ningbo.

Our relatives tried to persuade him not to quit. As they saw it, a job like that didn't come along often; he was taking home twice what most people in our town made, and working on the ships, there was always the opportunity to make contacts for work on the side. My father didn't explain his decision. He waved them off and vowed that he wasn't going back. Some of the relatives took my mother aside, but she could only say calmly, "Don't bother asking. It's no use."

He never returned to Ningbo. He took the money he made on the ships and opened a hotel, a seafood restaurant, and a gas station. It was a process of slow, steady failure. As each business failed, it was like he shed another layer of skin. He stopped looking after himself and became silent and moody. I was in my second year of high school when my father had his first stroke. He had just woken up from his afternoon nap and was about to go out to open the shop. He collapsed without warning, falling in the yard.

When my father was lying on his back in the hospital, about to go in for surgery, my mother finally asked, "Did something happen in Ningbo? Were you running away from something?"

My father grinned, showing his smoke-stained teeth.

"I knew it," my mother said flatly.

Today, only the southern half of the brick house my father built still stands.

When I go home, I always stop by for a look. The main part of the house was demolished, but the west wing, where my father stayed after his stroke, is still there, and so is the east wing, where my sister lived before she got married.

My father had two more strokes while living in the west wing of the old house. The paralyzed body in which he was trapped until he died was created in that house. It was in the east wing that my sister once cried while telling me the family was too poor for her to get married. She told me our family could never pay a dowry. She had already decided that she would marry a man as poor as her; she started ending friendships with friends who were better off.

I remember that night clearly. She went out with her boyfriend and came back alone. She was only gone about a quarter of an hour. She sneaked back into her room, making sure our parents didn't see her, then she pulled me aside. Her face was red. Her eyes were wet, but she did not let a single tear fall. It took her a long time to calm down enough to talk. She said, "You have to promise me you won't ask about him. If Mom and Dad ask, don't let them know what's going on."

I nodded.

Years later I found out that when my sister and her boy-friend went out that night, he had asked her, "What kind of dowry can your parents give?"

My mother finally rented out the old house to a family that moved to our town. She charged them 150 yuan a month, and the rent stayed the same for ten years. The tiny space was home to six people and a dog. They quickly removed any trace of my family or the way the house had once looked.

I went inside a few times not long after it had been rented out. After my father's stroke, he had sometimes fallen while trying to get around, leaving bloodstains on the floor; the blood had been covered by grease and grime. The space under the stairs that my father had carefully built for me as a playroom was filled with the odds and ends of the new tenants.

In those days, my mother also stopped by the old house, although I don't know if she was, like me, consciously looking for something, or if she was unwittingly drawn there.

Knowing my mother, I thought that she must have rented it to the family because she knew they would take it over. Only a family that big squeezed into the tiny house could fill the place with happiness and heartbreak.

The life of others painted in a thin coat over her own old life in the house was exactly what she needed. It provided just enough distance.

The newer four-story building where my mother lives now never felt like home to me.

That house was built when I was in my third year of high school, two years after my father had his first stroke. One day my mother called me into her room, opened the middle drawer of the table, and took out a roll of bills. She said we had one hundred thousand yuan. Some of it she had earned herself, some my sister earned as a bookkeeper, and some I had contributed from editing and tutoring. She told me that since I was the head of the household, I could decide what to do with it. Without really thinking, I told her we should keep saving.

During the two years my father had been unwell, my mother used to leave the house every night around eight or nine o'clock, carrying a cloth bag. Each time she came back from her nightly trip, I heard her toss something in the yard behind the house, and then she would come back in the house and pretend it was perfectly normal for her to be coming and going at that hour. My sister and I pretended not to know what was going on, but we already knew. She was secretly going each night to pick up the cabbage leaves, radish tops, and other discarded items from the floor of the market. She threw them in the yard and then in the morning washed them and cut off the rotten parts. She put them on the table without letting on where they had come from. Combined with four meatballs, the market scraps provided a meal. We didn't tell her we knew. We knew the truth, but we didn't want to face the consequences of revealing the lie.

That night, after I told her that I wanted to keep saving, she told me she wanted to build a house.

"Before your father got sick," she said, "he was talking about building a house. So that's what I want to do." That was her reasoning.

"But he still has medical bills," I said.

"I want to build a house," she said.

She was like a little girl in a toy store who refuses to budge from the aisle until her parents buy her the doll she wants.

I nodded. It would mean a few more years of eating vegetables of unknown origin. But I understood how she felt. I thought about the relatives who went out of their way to avoid us when we were in town or pretended we were invisible when we happened to make offerings at the ancestral temple at the same time.

I knew the house would be my mother's way of sending a message to the world. Once the house was built, she could hold her head high.

When the money was added up, there was enough to tear down half of the old house and put up a small two-story house. My mother picked an auspicious day to start construction and, despite not having completed elementary school, sketched a design for the new house. This was two weeks before I wrote my college entrance exam. Before the old house was torn down, the household was gripped by preparations, which saw family members shuffled around: my father and mother lived in the west wing of the old house, and my sister, who was old enough that our parents were waiting for the day she would get married and move out, had settled into the east wing. I had no place to live, so I moved into the school dormitory.

A week before the old house was to come down and work on the new house would begin, my mother insisted on buying a string of firecrackers. Whenever there was enough sun, she put the coil up on the roof to bake. She said that was the best way to make sure they went off with a clear, loud bang. That summer there were a few afternoons of inexplicably heavy rain. She would rush out as soon as the first drops of rain fell to take the firecrackers down, then bring them inside to dry off in front of an electric fan. She cared for her firecrackers like a mother does a newborn.

When demolition day came, one of the workers took a hammer and gave the wall a ceremonial tap. It was time. With all the neighbors watching, my mother went to the middle of the street, gently unrolled the string of firecrackers, and lit the fuse.

The sound was just as impressive as she had hoped. Blue-green smoke from the firecrackers floated up, mixing with dust from the road. As the smoke and noise filled the alley, I heard my mother exhale a long, deep sigh.


Building a house is a nerve-racking process, especially when you're going into debt to do it. My mother split her time between the gas station and the construction site. She was barely over a hundred pounds, but she put every last ounce of strength into her work. She went from moving around oil drums at the gas station to shouldering loads of bricks for the house. She trembled under the weight of the load, weaving between towers of bricks that stood as tall as her. And when that was done, she would rush over to the old house to look after my father.

With a mother like that, there was no way I could relax. When school let out, I rushed home to find her dripping with sweat—but she never stopped smiling. When she was tired, she would sit down right where she was and rest until she caught her breath. Even when she was completely exhausted, panting in the dirt, she never stopped smiling.

Whenever anyone walked by, no matter how exhausted she was, she would spring up to say, "That son of mine said he wants a new place for when he gets married. I kept telling him not to bother, but he insisted. What can I do? If he's going to be ambitious, I'd better support him."

My worst fear came true one afternoon a week before I took my exam. My mother was at work on the new house when she suddenly clutched her stomach and fainted. It didn't take long for the doctor to make a diagnosis: acute appendicitis.

By the time I made it to the hospital, the surgery was complete. I found her sitting up on a bed in the inpatient department on the second floor. She smiled when she saw me: "Is the foundation done yet?" She was worried I was going to yell at her.

I was about to lose my temper, but I was pulled up short

by the sound of shuffling, panting, and a cane tapping. It was my father. He had set off for the hospital as soon as he got the news. After hobbling out to the main road, he had managed to get a taxi, but the trip had still taken him three or four hours.

He shuffled into the room, leaning heavily on his cane, and then carefully lifted himself onto the other bed in the room. His long journey over, he breathed a sigh of relief. Still panting, he asked my mother, "You're okay?"

My mother nodded.

My father's mouth curled up as he tried to catch his breath and force the muscles in his face to cooperate. He asked again, "You're okay?" I could see that his eyes were red. "You're really okay?" His lips trembled like a small child on the verge of crying.

I stood there, silent.


By the time the house was done, I was away at university. It had taken six months to complete, and my mother had been forced to borrow money from my aunt and uncle. That was about all I knew, though, since she never told me how much they had lent her. I also knew that she owed the carpenter for his work on the gate. Every week, she counted up the money taken in at the gas station, took out the profits, and went to pay down her debts.

When it came time to move into the new house, my mother wanted to stay true to local traditions, which meant hosting a banquet for the relatives, even though it would cost her at least ten thousand yuan.

The night of the banquet, she couldn't stop smiling. When the guests had left, she got me and my sister to collect all the food that could be salvaged. I knew we would be eating leftovers for at least a week.

My sister was the first to protest. "Why are you spending money like crazy?" she asked.

My mother kept quiet and continued tidying up. But my sister had broken the silence, and I couldn't hold back anymore: "I don't even know how I'm going to pay next year's tuition."

"Why do you care so much what other people think?" my sister said. "What is he going to do if he can't pay for school? What about all the medical bills?" My sister began to weep.

My mother was silent for a long time. The only sound was my sister crying.

"You know what I live for?" my mother asked. "I live for this—that sigh of pride when it's all over, when we can hold our heads high. Nothing else matters but that."

It was the first time my mother had gotten angry at us since my father's stroke.


At the time, I was busy with school or working at the newspaper, and then tutoring during winter and summer breaks, so for me the new house remained temporary lodging.

My father, though, was quite satisfied with the new house. Since the left side of his body was paralyzed, he struggled to get around, but he went out each day to sit beside the gate and greet everyone as they passed. "Pretty amazing," he would say, "what that old wife of mine built, eh?"

His satisfaction was short-lived. I don't know who gave him the idea, but it was only about a week before he was heard saying to one of those passersby, "My wife isn't giving me money for my medical bills. She spent all the money building a house for our son, skimped on my treatment, and left me like this—I can't even walk."

Every time my mother went in or out, she was subjected to my father's vicious accusations. At first she pretended not to hear him, but gossip spread quickly in our small town. The fact that it was a disabled man leveling the accusations gave them even more weight.

One night, while I was away at university, Third Aunt called and told me to come home. My mother had called her that afternoon and said out of nowhere, "I want you to tell Blackie that I paid off most of the debts, but we still owe a bit. I don't want him to forget about the three thousand that's owed to Mr. Cai, the carpenter. These people helped us when we needed them, so I want him to look after them. Tell him that his father has to take his heart medicine every night around seven o'clock. He needs to make sure that he has at least a month of each prescription, and tell him, no matter what else is going on, he has to make sure his father takes his medicine. Let him know that I've saved up some money for his sister's dowry, then there's my jewelry, and the rest I hope she can come up with herself."

I got home as quick as I could. I saw that she had prepared a bowl of lean pork and ginseng soup. It was her favorite. She made it for herself whenever she was feeling sick. Whether it had any real medicinal qualities or was simply an effective placebo, she always felt better by the next day.

She heard me enter but said nothing.

I spoke first. "What are you doing?"

"I'm drinking soup," she said.

I looked at the soup in her bowl. It seemed thicker than normal. I guessed what was going on. I walked over, picked up the bowl, and took it away from her.

At that moment, even though neither of us said anything, we both knew what was happening.

She burst into tears as she watched me pour the soup down the drain. She said, "I don't want to give up. Do you think it was easy for me to get to this step? If I give up right now, it's humiliating."

That night revealed what had been lurking in both our hearts. Through the hard times, the idea of ending it all had floated like a malevolent spirit. Neither of us had dared talk about it, though.

I thought she was too fragile to hear those words, and she had thought the same of me.

But that night the ghost was made flesh.

My mother quietly led me upstairs to the room she shared with my father. He had gone to bed after dinner and was already fast asleep, his childlike snore echoing through the bedroom. My mother pulled open a drawer and took out a box. Inside the box was a paper bag wrapped in a scarf.

It was rat poison.

"I bought it after your father got sick," she said quietly. "There were so many times when I felt like I just couldn't take it anymore. I'd take out the poison. . . . I wanted to put it in the soup, but I couldn't do it, so I always put it back."

"I can't do it," I said. "I'm not willing. I don't believe things can't get better."

That night, I tried to convince her. I knew that since I was the head of the family, I could order her not to do it. Even for something like suicide, she needed my approval. She gave me her promise. She looked like a child. She sat beside me and began to cry.

I took the paper bag from her. I finally felt like the head of the family.

Even though I was the head of the household, I was still far from ready for the role. The week after I took the rat poison from my mother, my father lost his temper, and I took the bag out and screamed that it might be better if we all just died. Everyone stared at me. My mother forced the bag out of my hand, glared at me, and put it in her pocket.

In the days after the secret was revealed, the rat poison became one of my mother's tactics to defuse disputes in the house. Without speaking, my mother would climb the stairs to her bedroom, and whatever argument was taking place would be forgotten as we all sat silently, listening. At that moment all of the anger in our hearts slowly melted away, replaced by the thought of our mutual destruction. There was no way for us to be angry with that thought hanging over our heads.

The rat poison never served its true purpose of killing vermin, but it managed to snuff out all the anger and resentment that poverty and disability had visited on our family.

During my first year of university, when I was home for summer vacation, my mother called me into her room again. She took out a roll of bills.

"How about we put two more floors on it?" she said.

I couldn't decide whether to laugh or cry. It had taken three years of hard work to pay off our debts, and there were still times when I struggled to come up with money to pay my tuition—and my mother was about to go down the same road all over again.

My mother twisted the money nervously in her hands. Her face turned red. She looked like a general giving the order to dig in ahead of the final battle. "Nobody else around here has a four-story house," she said. "If we build one, we can finally hold our heads high."

I realized that my mother was even more stubborn than I

had first imagined. She didn't want merely to hold her head high—she wanted to be able to lord it over the neighbors.

I knew I couldn't refuse her.

Just as she had planned, the extra two stories on the house caused a stir. When the firecrackers went off to signal completion, my mother took my father on a walk to the market.

"You just wait a few more years," she said to everyone they passed. "My son and I are going to take down the old house in front, too. We'll have a little courtyard with a wall around it, and we'll put some effort into fixing the place up just right—we'll invite you over to have a look when we're done!"

"Come over and have a look when we're done," my father slurred, fighting his half-paralyzed tongue.

A year after that walk to the market my father suddenly passed away.

Two years later my mother went to the municipal government and saw the line cutting through her house.

On the way back from the municipal government office, she turned to me and asked, "Can we finish building it?"

"Sure," I said.

She tried to explain it to me: "Do you think I'm just being stubborn? I keep thinking, if it's going to be torn down, we should build more, spend more. . . . I don't know why I want to keep building."

She couldn't stop herself from crying. "I know," she said, "that if we hadn't built it, I'd be unhappy my whole life. It doesn't matter what house I ended up living in. It wouldn't matter where I ended up."

When we got home, we ate dinner and watched TV for a while, then my mother went to bed early. It was not her body that was tired but her heart. I couldn't sleep, though, so I crawled out of bed and turned on all the lights in the house. For the first time in years, I inspected every single part of the house. It was like seeing a face that was both familiar and strange; I ran my hand over the wrinkles, the age spots, and the scars. Not much care had gone into the top two stories of the house. They also lacked the special banisters my mother had installed for my father on the lower floors. There wasn't much furniture, either. The upper floors had stayed unoccupied until my father had passed away. Shortly afterward, my mother had abruptly moved upstairs; my room had been moved to the fourth floor then, too. For a while, my mother refused to set foot on the second floor.

The first room on the second floor had been my parents' bedroom. My room was right beside their room, and my sister's was across the hall. The second floor wasn't very big, less than a thousand square feet without the staircase to the balcony, and that tiny space was carved into three rooms. When my father was paralyzed and struggling to get around, he used to curse my mother for designing the place with no rhyme or reason. "I didn't even finish elementary school," my mother would say. "You think I had any qualifications as an architect?"

The marks of my father's cane on the walls of the second floor were still there. I opened the first room and found that it still held a faint scent of my father. The table that had once held my mother's money and the rat poison was still there, too, its top pockmarked from the times my father had angrily brought his cane down on it. I found the middle drawer locked. I had no idea what might be in there.

I left the lights off and went to sit in a chair beside the bed where my father once slept. I remembered how he lay there in the years after his stroke. I suddenly remembered something else, too: how I used to lie on his stomach when I was a boy.

The memory pulled me toward the bed, and once again I was enveloped by his scent. Pale moonlight lit the room. I felt something on his pillow and saw that it was a sticker portrait I had taken of myself at a photo booth many years before. My face looked startlingly pale. I took a closer look and realized that the picture had simply faded, rubbed smooth by my father's fingers stroking it.

I lay there for a while, motionless, fighting to choke down the sob that threatened to escape. I didn't want my mother to hear me. I swallowed my tears and ran from the second floor. I wanted to end that terrible quest. I was done exploring.

My mother woke me early the next morning. She had

discovered a team of municipal workers with surveying equipment. It reminded me of the times years before when she had come into my room to tell me, helplessly, that my father had fallen.

We watched them through the window for a while as they set up their instruments, went about their inscrutable business, then quickly jotted down figures in their notebooks. My mother said, "Looks like we'll have to hurry, huh?"


The afternoon after the surveyors came, my mother paid a visit to my uncle. Since my father had passed away, she had begun going to him for advice. She also knew he had some connections with construction companies, so he could get her a good price on the work that remained on the house.

I stayed home, but restless anxiety sent me eventually to the fourth-story roof. The house was built at one of the highest points in the village, and from the roof I could see the entire town laid out below me.

I had never noticed before that the entire town seemed full of construction sites. Seen from above, the construction sites and excavation pits in the red soil looked like oozing sores and bloody gashes. A highway under construction in the east had the sinister appearance of some massive beast snaking across the landscape. All along the new road were houses in various states of demolition; the scaffolding and dust-proof netting that covered them gave them the appearance of smashed limbs wrapped in splints and gauze. I knew the house I was standing on would soon join them, as would many others. In another year or two, this scene would be even more grim, flayed raw like a prisoner's backside.

I tried to imagine all the stories that had taken place in the homes I could see below me. How many traces were left of the souls that had once occupied them? All the sadness and happiness of years gone by—they would be reduced to dust floating over the ruins.

It occurred to me that I treated my heart just like municipal planning officials had treated the town: in the name of development, in the name of building toward some future goal, in the name of respectability, I had been in a hurry to redevelop, demolish, and rebuild everything I held dear. There was no going back, for me or for the town.

When my uncle came over that evening, my mother hurried to greet him, thinking he had found her a company to work on the house.

When the tea was ready, he took a sip and paused for a moment to savor it. He said, "I don't think you should build it."

My mother demanded an explanation. He refused to give her one. "I just can't figure it out," he said angrily. "You said you wanted to build a house for Blackie. You said it was so your family could hold their heads high—I can understand that, but what's the point now?"

I tried to help my mother explain it to him, but he refused to listen. "I'm opposed to the idea," he said. "Don't bother trying to convince me." He changed the topic, suggesting I buy a place in Beijing. "Don't be so selfish," he said to my mother. "You have to think about your son."

My mother's face turned red as she tried to hold back her emotions.

"Well," he said, feeling uncomfortable, "I'm willing to listen, if you want to tell me what you've got in mind."

But my mother did not speak.

"It was actually my idea to keep building," I said.

I didn't want to explain it to him, but I could understand why my mother wanted to keep building. Even though I had become the nominal head of the family after my father's stroke, he had never really given up the position. It was his family; he started it.

It took me until that day to understand my mother's real intentions. She had not been building for herself, or even for me. It wasn't about being able to hold our heads high. She was doing it for my father, the man who had brought us together. She wanted his family to be strong; she wanted the family to be complete.

Even though she could never say it out loud, this was the way my mother expressed her love.

My uncle couldn't understand why I was supporting my mother's idea, but he agreed to respect my decision. I knew he had practical concerns about my future. The idea of building under the almost assured threat of demolition was absurd, and I knew there was no way I could honestly explain it to him.

With his help, my mother found a construction team

and made hasty preparations. She prayed over the right date to begin work. It would be a week from then, and I would already be back in Beijing.

The afternoon before I left, I took my mother to the bank to withdraw money. When she had the bills in her hand, she immediately sat down to count and recount them. That money was a treasure won through years of struggle and poverty. She tucked the stack of bills against her breast and carried it home like a newborn.

It should have been a happy day for her, but she grumbled the whole way home. "I'm sorry," my mother said, as we walked down the alley toward the house. "If we do this, you'll never have the money to buy a place in Beijing."

I could only laugh.

And then she finally summoned the courage to say what was really on her mind: "There's something I've been meaning to ask you, but I'm worried it'll upset you. You know the most important thing for a house in our town is the stone tablet beside the gate, right? I want to know if you would mind putting your father's name on it."

"I don't mind," I said. I didn't want her to know what I felt at that moment. So many things I had long suspected were proven to be true. I fought to hold back tears. "Actually," I said, "I think you should keep the stone that Father put above the gate of the old house, the couplet with your two names."

I saw a smile slowly spread across her face. Her middle-aged face had the expression of a shy teenager. I reached out and stroked her cheek. I said to myself, "This sweet mother of mine."

That year, all of my coworkers who were back in Beijing for the first workday after the Spring Festival break went out together. Over a table in the noisy dining room, everyone told their stories about going home to visit family for the new year: waiting in line two days to buy train tickets, the new unfamiliarity of home, the growing gap between parent and child. . . . Someone suggested a toast to all those faraway hometowns.

I raised my cup. I gave an unspoken toast to my coworkers: Do whatever it takes to be happy, you lonely souls and wild ghosts.

And then the thought of my mother and her house came to mind.

Even if the house was demolished, even if I could never afford a place in Beijing, I would always have a family to go back to.

# 3

# Frailty

I knelt to light the gold paper, and my two cousins helped him step across the flame. The burning paper was a ceremony meant to cleanse the soul. All bad luck and spiritual pollution would be swept away and deposited safely outside the doorway. And that is how my father returned home from the hospital, where he had been recovering from a stroke. It was about ten o'clock at night.

Our local Hokkien custom dictated that the relatives—both distant and close—stop by our home for a visit. They paraded up to the house, each one offering supplements and snacks they thought might help his condition, and then proffering their solemn vows to help my father in any way they could. Some of the men started reminiscing with my father about old times, the glory days, ripping and running together. Some of the relatives brought up times when my father had helped them out of a jam and thanked him again. And a few of the women couldn't help themselves and wrapped their arms around my father, sobbing.

My father seemed distant. He let the women cry. He would have preferred to go back to reminiscing about old times. "What are you crying for?" he asked a woman who had broken down in tears. "I'm back, right? It's nothing."

But my father's tongue was still partially paralyzed from the stroke. When he spoke, all that came out was a string of slurred syllables. He paused and looked around, then he laughed, showing his smoke-stained teeth. Everyone laughed along with him.

It seemed like a fairly good start.

The reception went on until one in the morning. The stream of well-wishers slowed to a trickle, and when all of the relatives had finally come and gone, my mother and I each supported a shoulder to help him to the bathroom. We looked like two movers trying to lift a grand piano. We labored under his weight, huffing and puffing the whole way.

We had to stop a few times, and my mother laughed and said, "You didn't miss any meals in there, did you? You somehow managed to gain weight!" I couldn't help but think to myself, how many times a day will we have to make the same trip, dragging him to and from the bathroom? I started to wonder exactly how we would live from then on.

It was no easy feat getting my father back to bed. There was plenty of time to make small talk, but it felt like an unspoken tension lingered between us. During the three months my father had been in the hospital, first in Quanzhou and then in Fuzhou, I had only seen him a few times when I was home from school. I barely recognized the man my two cousins helped out of the car that night. His head had been shaved for surgery. He looked deflated. It wasn't that his arms were thinner or he'd lost his belly; he just looked like the air had been let out of him.

Since he came in the door, during the two hours while he received our relatives, I had been studying him. I was trying to find some trace of my father in that hunchbacked stranger. When he spoke, it was not with my father's voice. My father had a booming voice, and he cursed fluently at the slightest provocation. The paralysis on his left side had affected his mouth, so he slurred his words, and the effort of speaking left him exhausted. The rowdy, larger-than-life man in the stories the relatives told—I couldn't find him.

He broke the silence first. "You okay?" he slurred.

I nodded.

He smiled. "Don't worry. Give me another month and I'll be back to normal."

I nodded. I opened my mouth to speak, but I wasn't sure what to say. I knew in my heart that it was impossible.

"That motorbike has been sitting there for too long. When I get better, I'll buy you a new one. We can ride up the coast, feel the wind in our hair! You can take your sister. Your mom can ride with me."

That trip up the coast had been our only trip together as a family. My father wanted to step backward to the time when he had been the pillar of the family.

The morning after returning home from the hospital, he fell for the first time.

My mother was out shopping when it happened. I heard a muffled thud from his room. I jumped out of bed and ran to check on him. He had fallen to the floor and was as helpless as a baby. When he saw me, he tried to mutter some explanation. He hadn't come to terms with his own condition. He wasn't ready to become a man who struggled to get out of bed. He had sat up and tried to swing his legs to the floor, but his paralyzed left side hadn't kept up with the rest of his body. He had ended up tipped over and crashed to the floor. As he tried to explain, I saw tears gather at the corners of his eyes. His body was no longer under his control, and neither were his tears.

He wasn't used to his body. I wasn't used to him crying. I rushed to help him, trying not to let our eyes meet. I tried to pull him to his feet, but he outweighed me by seventy or eighty pounds. He did his best, putting every last ounce of strength into helping his son. But it was a lost cause.

I knew it, and he knew it, too. The disease hung like an anchor around his neck. He laughed and said, "I guess I did get fat, huh? Don't worry. Give me some time. I'll figure it out."

He slowly and carefully got his right leg under him and then managed to get himself upright. He teetered for a moment, looking like a high-rise with its foundation knocked out, then he tilted precariously to the right and collapsed to the floor.

I panicked and rushed to grab him, but gravity won, and we both toppled to the floor.

We lay together on the floor for a long time, trying to catch our breath, neither of us moving, neither of us speaking, neither of us knowing what to say.

Finally my father looked over at me and tried to force the disobedient muscles in his face into a smile. Even if he had been able to, his face would have betrayed how he really felt. That smile . . . I don't think I'll ever be able to put it into words.

After that, I began to put myself in his shoes. I tried to imagine what it would be like to find my own body unresponsive to my commands. I wanted to experience it myself, so that I could better look after him.

When I smiled at someone, I tried to hold the left side of my face rigid, so that I could see the shock and horror of the person I was smiling at. I wanted to experience the same embarrassment my father must have felt. I thought about what I would say to make the situation less awkward. When I was eating, I tried to imagine what it would be like to struggle with a pair of chopsticks. When I went out for a walk, I practiced walking with my left leg stiff and immobile. I fell a lot. I was bruised black and blue. But I realized that my father's numb left side wouldn't even have been able to feel those cuts and scrapes.

In the days after my father returned home, the members of the family slowly fell into their roles. It was as if we were staging a play with no access to the script. We only had a general idea what the play was about. We knew that we had to express some type of optimism. We were all trying to convince each other that things were getting better. We muddled our way through, improvising our lines, trying to figure out exactly what parts we were playing.

My mother was cast in the role of the unflappable wife who never let on how she suffered. When my father had an accident in bed, she would laugh and tease him. "Look at you! Like a little kid again!" After her laughter abruptly ended, she would take the sheets out into the alley to wash them. The joke wasn't funny, but she had to keep telling it. When she finished her tasks at home, she went out to watch over the gas station, which, before it closed, provided our family with a livelihood.

My elder sister was a perceptive girl. She stayed by our father's side and tried her best to take care of anything she thought he might need. She cooked for him, fed him, and massaged the numb left side of his body. Since my father's illness had forced him to temporarily abandon his post as head of household, my mother picked up most of the slack, and my sister got the rest.

And my role, I knew, was to take over as head of the family. I felt like a politician on the campaign trail. Even when my constituents' concerns went unspoken, I could still read their expressions and the true states of mind that those expressions were sometimes deployed to conceal. I read their faces and gave them whatever I thought they needed. I put in carefully calculated appearances and gave them a share of my time and effort. I was sometimes forced to rule on the family's various disagreements, swooping in to rap my gavel and offer judgment. Whatever the content of the ruling, I knew it had to be delivered with confidence. When I ruled, I felt like an actor again, delivering a forceful monologue to a rapt audience.

We were all actors, and we played our roles the best we could, but each of us felt how unnatural the whole production would have seemed to an outside observer. It was all so cheap and tawdry—more comedy than drama perhaps. None of us were professional actors, after all, and we were all frustrated and dissatisfied with the roles we had been cast in.

But the show had to go on. Even if we were playing to only one spectator, that spectator was life. Life does not sit quietly in its seat and take in the show; instead it jeers and glares like a harsh director, never satisfied, always quick to throw another plot twist into the script, demanding that we dig deep for our true motivation.

My mother fell while trying to move an oil drum at the gas station. She used to help my father with them, tipping over the several-hundred-pound drums, then rolling them away for storage. But with him confined to bed, she was forced to attempt it by herself. She had set her shoulder to a drum and was leaning the entire weight of her slim frame against it. The drum wouldn't budge an inch. That day, when I got out of school, I headed to the gas station, as I usually did. I saw her squatting in the oily mud of the yard, sobbing. The director had called for action, but I had no idea what my lines were. I pretended not to see her and rushed home instead.

Meanwhile, my father had lost his temper with my sister for not getting his dinner ready fast enough. As soon as she saw me come in the door, she pulled me aside. She couldn't tell me what had happened. All she could do was mutter angrily.

In the end, it was my father who yelled "cut." Two weeks had passed since he had returned home. He had tried many times to test the limits of his body, but each trial had been a failure. My mother came home looking exhausted, her hair disheveled. Without speaking, she put a cane down beside my father. He looked at the cane, and he saw his future. His frustration got the better of him. He picked up the cane and swung it angrily at his wife.

Thanks to the paralysis, his aim was off. He didn't land a solid blow but still managed to raise a bruise and knock her to the floor.

The next scene in the drama was my sister shrieking, my angry shouts, and my father's hysteria. Finally, we collapsed in each other's arms, all of us weeping.

What the hell kind of story is this? That was the question I asked after I had helped my mother to bed and got my sister calmed down, prepared my father's dinner, helped him wash, led him back to his room, and then retreated to my own bedroom. I was asking thin air.

I don't know if I expected anyone to answer me. I looked around and then asked another question: How does this story end?

There was no response. I didn't expect one.

My father came up with his own solution to the problem. That solution relied not on objective facts but on his own peculiar logic. He had decided that his goal should be to nurse his body back to full health, then resume his role as the head of the family.

But I knew there was a fatal flaw in his way of thinking: there was no way he could ever go back to what he had once been. He had had two cerebral embolisms after parts of his heart valve broke loose and became lodged in his brain's circulation. The blockage—a piece of the heart valve—in his brain could not be dissolved, and there was no way it could be flushed out, either, since it would likely become lodged in another part of his brain, which could leave another part of his body paralyzed. His old body was lost forever to him. The truth was cruel. I understood the gravity of the situation.

I even went to the library to look up a picture of the heart valve. It's a miniscule thing that looks a lot like the mouth of a fish, opening and closing as the heart ventricles contract. That tiny piece of internal equipment had malfunctioned and left half of my father's body paralyzed.

I knew that the longer my father persisted in that way of thinking, the worse it would be for him when he finally realized the truth. But I wasn't ready to try dissuading him; I didn't have any better ideas.

Even if his logic was flawed, it was at least hopeful. And hope was what kept the family going.

One autumn night after he returned home, he called me over and explained his plan. He told me that he knew the left side of his body was locked up because a blood vessel was blocked, so, he said, "if I start moving around and get my blood flowing, the old blood will get washed away, and I can get my left side moving." I pretended to believe him, and he seemed to be fooled by my performance.

Since his end goal was complete recovery, he was able to accept the cane as a temporary aid. The next day, he went out for a walk to Winding Road Market. He wanted to see how long it would take him to get there. When he didn't come back for lunch, the three of us split up and went looking for him. We found him sitting at a street corner not far from home. I made the journey that had taken him all morning in about twenty minutes.

But he considered it a good beginning. "At least I know where I'm starting from," he told me.

The next day, he laid out his scheme in detail: he planned to go out every morning at eight o'clock, walk to where we had found him the day before, then return home in time for lunch at twelve; after lunch, he would take his nap, then go out again at around half past one, heading for the Winding Road Market, leaving enough time to make it back for dinner at seven; and then after dinner, he would work on balance and exercise his left foot.

Even now, looking back, I am grateful to my father for being so strong. That might have been our happiest time together. Even if it was going to end in tragedy, his dream of making himself whole again became our collective fantasy.

My mother followed his schedule with strict devotion. She made sure each meal had eggs or meat, just as he had asked. He said that eggs and meat would keep him strong.

He used to say that when he was working on the ships and moving heavy cargo, he sometimes got so exhausted that he was on the verge of collapse, but once he got a good meal with meat or eggs in him, he was ready to go again.

Each night, when everyone returned home, we did his exercises along with him, turning it into a sort of competition. Intentionally or not, my father always won these improvised games. We all went to bed happy.

We enjoyed those fleeting moments of happiness because they were all we had. Before my father's two strokes, there had been a heart surgery and four stays in the hospital—and that was just the beginning. Even with the help of our relatives, we were slowly going broke.

We had missed out on a rare opportunity when Petro-China offered to buy out the gas station. The offer came just before my father got sick, and since we were focused on his health, we let it slip. Even if the PetroChina offer had never come, we should have tried to expand and upgrade the gas station, but we ended up missing our chance there, too. When the large gas station near the estuary opened up, there was no way we could compete with its state-of-the-art facilities. The station near the estuary even had a shop to pick up snacks and drinks while filling up.

Nonetheless, with our savings almost gone, we knew we had to reopen the gas station. Even if we didn't have the facilities or the snacks that the bigger station had, we had a secret weapon: my mother and her inimitable way with people. She always knew the right thing to say; the neighbors admired her. People would come by just to visit her, then fill up their tanks almost as an afterthought.

Whether it was the result of a formal pact or not I could not say, but the neighbors seemed to band together to support our station, even though they would have told you that the station near the estuary was much nicer. Things at our station ran at a slower pace. Everything was still done by hand, my mother would often struggle to make change or calculate a bill, and it was not rare for customers to arrive and find nobody working, since my mother often had to rush home to make my father's lunch, make sure he took his pills, and wash his clothes. Our customers were willing to wait.

Once business picked up, my sister and I started pitching in at the station, too. We took shifts when my mother was busy at home. We started with simple tasks, like filling big soda bottles with fuel, since when motorcycles came to fill up it was easier to use the bottles than pump from a drum. Then we would move the drums and do any of the other heavy lifting that my mother couldn't handle.

We did our best, but sometimes we weren't around to help her, like when the flatbed trucks came by to fill up and she had to move an entire drum of fuel by herself. The big trucks took a full drum, which was good for the bottom line but meant a lot of work for my mother. One time, while trying to drag a drum over to a truck, she gave up halfway and broke down crying. The driver's mother, who was in her sixties, took pity on my mother and helped her drag the drum, covering herself in grease in the process. After that incident, the flatbed drivers made sure to come by after five o'clock, when they knew my sister and I would be there to help.

When the sun went down, my sister and I rolled away the barrels, closed up shop, and went home to accompany my father on his nightly workout. We went to bed completely exhausted but fell asleep with smiles on our faces.

I threw myself into the work and the exercises. I wanted to deny that everything would end in tragedy. I didn't want to think about the suffering that was awaiting us.

And we did manage to put some money away. That was a relief. The thing about poverty is that the lack of money doesn't just wear you down; it's almost as if other people can smell it on you. When you're poor, even if nobody bears you any ill will, they start to drift away, or they go out of their way to avoid you. They are worried that you will drag them under, too.

My mother felt it most deeply.

She was a proud woman, allergic to even the slightest expression of sympathy. When she sensed that some neighbors were coming to the gas station out of charity, she gave them a chilly reception and made sure they never came back.

I remember one day when I unexpectedly found my mother shut up in her room. She told me that a man had come by the station. "He asked how your father was doing," she said, "so I told him he was fine." The man laughed and told my mother that he used to run with the same gang as my father had, although he had been mostly a hanger-on.

"You never know how things are going to end up, huh?" the man said, then jerked a thumb at his car. "Look how the two of us turned out, right?" He meant my father and him.

My mother got upset and knocked over the drum she was pumping from. "We're closed," she said.

"Hey," the man said angrily, "I'm here to help you out—where do you get off acting like that?"

My mother picked up a stone and, without really thinking, threw it at the side of his car. It ricocheted off a door panel with a thud. The man saw the gouge in the paint job and lunged at her. She took off running, tears running down her face, then grabbed a bigger rock and started chasing him. She hit him solidly in the head with the rock, leaving blood running down his face.

She didn't stick around to see what he would do. She ran for her life. When she got home, she bolted the iron gate, locked the front door, then went to take shelter in her bedroom. That was where she was, still sobbing, when I got home.

"I was just so angry," she said to me by way of explanation. She looked like a child sent home from school trying to explain what she had done wrong.

She might have been angry, but what the man had said stung her in some deeper way, too.

I went with my mother to the gas station. After she ran away, nobody was left to look after it, so we expected the worst. We mentally prepared ourselves to see all the fuel stolen, the place trashed or maybe even burned. We both knew that the loss of the gas station, even if it was temporary, was a blow our family might not recover from.

We were like contestants on a game show about to see the final result announced. My mother covered her eyes.

Everything was where it should be. All the fuel was accounted for. Even the table and chair in the station's small office hadn't been moved. Someone had placed an empty gas can on the table, beside a hundred-yuan note to cover the cost of the fuel.

We were speechless. We sat together and laughed, breathing in the thick smell of gasoline. We stayed there until my mother remembered she had to make dinner. We ran home together.

I know it wasn't the typhoon's fault. Fate had already decided our fate. All that was left to be decided was what form disaster would come in. But it took the weight off to put the blame on something we were powerless over. To this day, I still curse that typhoon.

Southern Fujian has no shortage of typhoons. This typhoon was not the first we had been through. When a typhoon warning was received, everyone set about preparing, patching things up, nailing down anything that might blow away, and stopping up leaky roofs. Then they would shut all the doors and windows and hunker down to ride it out. At night, the windows would rattle in the wind, but that was about as bad as it ever got. Safe inside, looking out, the typhoon seemed like nothing but a 4D movie the heavens put on for us Hokkien people once a year.

I wasn't the type of kid to sit at home and watch life go by, so I liked to go out and try my luck against the typhoon. Back then, the wind and the rain were still clean; now if you went out in a typhoon, you might end up soaked with chemicals. When I heard the typhoon coming, I would open the door and yell a challenge, then run outside, letting the wind and rain crash against me. When I made it back inside, I would have to face my mother scolding me for getting completely soaked.

For me, the typhoons were just another happy memory in a happy childhood. That came to an end that year, though.

Even before the typhoon came, my father had started to notice that things were not moving in a hopeful direction. That summer, no matter how much he exercised, his left arm remained paralyzed, trapped against his chest. He could still control his left knee, but there was no tangible improvement. And—this is what really scared him—he had begun to lose feeling in his toes. My sister used to wait for him to drift off to sleep, then cut his toenails. That year she slipped once and cut the flesh of his toe. My sister ran to get a bandage to stanch the trickle of blood, but my father didn't even wake up. In the morning, he was shocked to discover a ball of gauze wrapped around his toe.

Frustration, like an advancing army, slowly took over, capturing him piece by piece. He tried not to let on what he was feeling; we pretended not to notice.

He knew what was coming. The sadness he concealed was like a wound that had become infected. It was spreading, slowly making his life unbearable, and there would soon come a day when he could no longer keep it hidden. He clung to his schedule even more tenaciously. He had my mother put a clock in his room and another in the main room, so that he could always keep an eye on the time. As soon as he woke up in the morning, he would yell for my mother, then he would point up at the clock. He set a time limit of fifteen minutes to get up and dressed. Within twenty minutes, he wanted to be washing his face. Within thirty minutes, he wanted to be on his way downstairs. Within fifty minutes, he wanted his breakfast done, and five minutes later, he wanted to be on the toilet; and he would be out the door by eight o'clock. But then he would complain about being one or two minutes slower here and there. . . .

He sometimes flew into a rage and swept everything off the table or took his cane and rapped it on the floor, shouting, "You don't want me to get better, do you? You don't want me to get better?"

My father, it seemed, feared that as slowly as my mother

worked, she would always fall behind his schedule, and he would never be able to recover the paralyzed half of his body.

It was around then that the first typhoon of autumn arrived. We spent the afternoon before it arrived inspecting the house in preparation for the storm. It would be the first typhoon when we were all together since my father got sick. According to the weather forecast, it was to be one of the biggest typhoons in years, and it was set to make landfall in our town.

I saw a reporter from the state broadcaster announcing that the Ministry of Civil Affairs had arrived to coordinate the disaster response, but he seemed a bit underwhelmed by the storm. He had probably arrived in the province hoping to file a report while being battered by gale-force winds and blasted by torrential rain, clinging to a tree to steady himself while shouting to the anchor over the roar of the storm.

He wouldn't have to wait long to get his wish. That was merely the calm before the storm.

The wind started to blow, kicking up whirlwinds that seemed to dance down the road, and then, just after one in the afternoon, the tempest struck. Rain came like a volley of gunfire, leaving dimples in the dusty road. As the wind began to howl, the TV reporter shouted to the anchor.

My mother was already home, since she knew nobody

was going to stop by the gas station, and my father was back from his morning exercise. When I got up to close the door, he yelled for me to stop. "What are you shutting the door for?" he asked.

"Typhoon's coming," I said. "Everything'll get wet in here."

"Leave it open. I'm going out."

"In a typhoon?"

"I have to exercise."

"In the middle of a typhoon?"

"You don't want me to get better. I have to exercise."

"Why not take a day off?"

"You don't want me to get better."

My father got up from the table where his lunch sat untouched, picked up his cane, and headed for the door.

I wanted to grab the cane from him, but he saw me coming and smacked me across the arm with it, leaving a purple welt. My mother stood up to go to the door, but my father pushed past her. With his cane in his right hand to keep his balance, he had only his weak left hand free to work the knob.

Failing to open the door, he started to beat on it with his cane, crying and cursing. "None of you want me to get better," he said. "None of you! You don't want me to get better."

My father's voice reminded me of a tractor tipped on its side, its engine roaring. The neighbors heard him and started cracking their windows to look out.

I went to the door and flung it open. "Go," I said, "just go. Nobody's stopping you."

My father didn't even glance at me. Balancing his awkward bulk on the cane, he headed out the door. The wind and rain seemed to intensify at that moment. He was blown clear across the road, as if he weighed no more than a leaf.

When I saw him splayed on the road, struggling to rise to his feet, I rushed to his side. He was still angry. He pushed me away, and I watched him try again to get his feet under him, before finally giving up and collapsing limply to the ground.

My mother went over and, without saying a word, leaned against his left side and helped him slowly get to his feet. She tried to lead him toward the house, but he pushed her aside and hobbled in the other direction.

There was nothing but the wind and rain and my father's trembling body, tiny and powerless, struggling like a bird in a storm. Our neighbors came out and tried to call to him, telling him to go home, but he seemed not to hear them. He kept walking.

As he walked by a gap between two buildings, a gust of wind came down the alley like a cannon, knocking him to the ground again.

When some of the neighbors went over to help him up, he pushed them away. He did not want their help, but there was no way he could get back to his feet by himself. He kept going, crawling on his belly like a lizard. When he could go no farther, he let one of the neighbors drag him to his feet and help him home. He didn't stay there long. At four o'clock, he was ready to go out again.

Despite the typhoon, he was committed to his schedule. He repeated the same pattern three times.

The next day, with the typhoon still blowing, my father stayed in bed. He refused to talk. He lay in bed looking frustrated and helpless.

He would not say it himself, but I knew that something had snapped inside of him. The sense of defeat seemed to hang in the air—I could smell it even, a salty smell, like the breath of the ocean.

He stayed in his bed as if he had been born there and would die there.

After a few days, he broke his silence and called me to his bedside. "Can you take me out along the coast on your motorcycle?" he asked me.

That afternoon, the whole family pitched in to get him on the motorbike and then tie the two of us together with a length of cloth.

The low autumn sunlight was as white as snow, as white as salt. The sea shone magnificently under its pure light as I drove along the levee. We watched a kid roasting sweet potatoes over some coals, a few teenagers who had drunk their fill and were taking turns smashing the empty liquor bottles against a wall, and fishermen headed out with rakes and wicker baskets.

My father was silent while we drove. I searched in vain for a topic of conversation. "That guy that waved to us from the boat, he used to be in your gang, right?" I asked. "I heard that you guys used to be the toughest crew around here."

He was so quiet I worried for a second that he had fallen off the back of the bike. He was as quiet as a potted plant.

He finally spoke when we got home. "Okay," he said, "I'm ready."

I knew what he meant. He was telling me that he was ready to die.

The disease had finally conquered him. He was like a prisoner on death row, resigned to his fate.

But it was only by giving up all hope that he could finally make peace with the reality of his illness.

He no longer had to pretend to be strong. He could give in to his emotions. He would sometimes break down when his left arm refused to respond. He gave up on his schedule and his exercises and his rules. Instead, he went each day and sat by the front gate. When people walked by that he didn't like, he didn't hold back from shouting abuse at them. When the neighbors' dogs came around, he would swing his cane at them to drive them off. When the local kids got in his way when he was out and about, he pushed them out of the way with the cane, too. He no longer had to hold on to his identity as family patriarch. He acted more like a child—a bratty, spoiled child.

I would arrive home after school to find my father sitting in front of our house with some of the older men of the neighborhood. They sat around him, listening to his only slightly exaggerated stories of the glory days. They occasionally even wiped away a few tears with him. Every now and then, we would get complaints from neighbors about him upsetting children and pets.

He was no longer the man I had once called my father. My sister and I no longer called him Father, but switched to his nickname, A-Yuan. When my niece was born, he called her Little Kernel (in Hokkien it means something like "plump and cute"), so people started to call him Big Kernel.

He liked the nickname. He continued to weep with the old men and fight with the local dogs.

Death, for whatever reason, seemed unwilling to come for him.

That did not deter him from constantly delivering what sounded to me like deathbed testaments. He used to say, "You need to make sure you choose the right woman to marry. I won't be around to help you." He told me, "I want you to cremate me, so you can carry a piece of me around with you wherever you go." After a few days, he started to say, "Don't worry, when I'm gone, the family will still be here."

I usually tried to laugh it off, chalking it up to my father coping with his illness and his inevitable end. But that cut me deep. When he said again, "Don't worry, when I'm gone, the family will still be here," I couldn't take it anymore.

"You can't talk like that!" I yelled.

"It's the truth."

"But don't say it again."

He left it at that. But later, when he went out to sit by the gate, he started telling everyone who passed, "I just told my son, when I'm gone, the family will still be here. He got angry at me. I still think I'm right."

Then he'd turn to look at me to see if I was angry enough to go over and shout at him again.

At first I couldn't accept my father regressing. I couldn't understand how he could strip off his patriarchal identity. And the man-child that he became was quite strange. His words still held the weight of life and death for me, but he never held back from speaking. However I felt about the change, though, I knew it was the best way for him to live out his days.

My father might have been waiting for death, but he seemed to experience a sort of rebirth, taking sudden pleasure in life again. He talked about death like an old friend who would be stopping by to visit sometime in the distant future. He sometimes seemed to forget that vague date. "My boy," he said, "when you have a kid, are you going to raise him in our town?" And another time he asked me if he could name my future child.

"I thought you were about to die," I said, teasing him.

"You're right," he said, as if he had suddenly come to his senses. "I might as well just hurry up and die." Then he laughed so hard that drool leaked from the left side of his crooked mouth.

I learned a few things during my father's long illness that I expect most people do not know. One of them is that when it gets cold in the winter, blood vessels start to contract, and it's particularly tough on older people, since their circulation tends to be weaker. The same goes for anyone who has paralysis after a stroke, since vasoconstriction makes hemiplegia even worse.

When the cold weather came, my father found it even harder to walk, to the point that his left foot seemed to completely disobey his commands. He fell often, ending up covered in bruises, with a gash in his head. I used my authority as head of the family to order him to stay home. I felt like a father giving orders to a disobedient child.

He listened, then looked up at me, blinking, and said, "If I'm good, will you buy me some of my marinated duck?"

It was an unexpectedly cold winter, colder than any winter I remembered, colder than a southern Fujian winter had any right to be. The chill seemed to penetrate right to the bone marrow. When I went out, I could feel my scalp tightening as the cold wind scraped my bare head. I bought a hat and a parka for my father. He had always been heavy-set, but in his winter clothes, he looked like a meatball. The Big Kernel nickname had never seemed more appropriate.

Even though we kept him bundled up, he started to have fainting spells. The first one happened while he was eating. He was halfway through his meal when he suddenly slumped down, his face buried in his hand. He managed to get out that he was feeling light-headed, and then his eyes rolled back in his head and he started to foam at the mouth.

My mother jumped up and rushed to his side, pinching the skin between his nose and upper lip in the hope that the pressure point would rouse him. She shouted for my sister to get some warm water. I rushed to get the doctor.

"I really thought I was going to die," he said when he came to. He sighed. "I guess I wasn't ready to go."

"Then stay here," I said, taking him in my arms. I held him for a long time.

The good news was that my father was afraid to die. But the doctor had some bad news. He told us that as time went by, as my father grew older, his circulation would worsen, so that the paralysis on his left side would slowly become more severe. He might be rendered incontinent, confined to his bed.

That night, after we received the news, my mother took me aside. As she figured it, probably within five years, my father would be bedridden. "Don't worry about me," she told me. "I can shoulder the burden." She had calculated that if my father lived to be eighty years old, taking into account his medical care and prescription fees, the living expenses for the two of them, and what it would cost to get me married, it would cost a fortune.

"I don't want you to worry," my mother said. "We're in this together. Even if your father is completely paralyzed, I'll be there for him. I can pick up some small jobs again, things I can do at home. All you need to do is work as hard as you can for these five years."

When it came time for me to leave, my father behaved like a child, begging me not to go. He very reluctantly agreed to let me go to Beijing to look for a job. The plan my mother and I agreed on called for us to work as hard as we could for the next five years, so once I had a job, I would only come home a couple of times a year. Every time I went back, I brought my work with me, so I usually only saw my father briefly before retreating to my room to write. In the morning, he would call me for breakfast. He was dying to see me. But I had usually been up until five or six in the morning writing, so I would drowsily stumble down, yell at him not to bother me, then stumble back upstairs to sleep. The same pattern would repeat itself the next day.

I worked that way for three years, and I was honestly surprised to check my bank account one day and realize that I had saved two hundred thousand yuan. I started to fantasize about what I could do with the money. I never told my father this, but I had an idea that I could take him to America to see a doctor. I had heard about some advances in nano-neuroscience, where microscopic tools could be threaded into blood vessels in the brain to clear blockages.

I started to cut my expenses, carefully adding up every yuan I spent. When I got home at night, I checked my account online, watching the number slowly go up as the days went by.

I told my mother about my savings, but I kept my plan from her. She was just happy that she no longer had to struggle to get by. Another three years, I thought to myself, and my father will be better again. Once my father got better, he could return to sit at the head of the family, and everything would be like it once was.

But all that changed one rainy afternoon. As I paused on the street to watch a monitor showing the countdown to the World Cup opening ceremonies, my phone rang with a call from my cousin.

"Can you talk right now?" he asked.

"Sure! But I thought you'd be watching the World Cup. You're a soccer fan, right?"

"Forget about that. I need to talk to you. I want you to promise that when you hear what I have to say you won't panic."

"What's going on? Why are you talking like that?"

"Can you promise me?"

"Sure. Okay."

"Your father passed away. It was just after four o'clock. When your mother got home, she saw he'd fallen. He passed out again. She called us over to drive him to the ER, but on the way there, he passed."

I swore at my father, *I thought you still wanted to live?*

*You said you wanted to live. You broke your promise.*

I flew into Xiamen and got home just after eleven that night. I found my father laid out in front of the ancestral altar. He still looked plump, but his face seemed to wear a grimace of dissatisfaction. The cheers of neighbors watching the World Cup came from houses along the alley. Every four years, I thought, the whole world joined together to celebrate. None of them realized that I had just lost the most important person in my life.

I took my father's hand. I couldn't cry.

His hand was stiff and cold. I couldn't suppress the anger that rushed up from somewhere inside of me. "How could you do this?" I yelled at him. "Without even saying goodbye, you just leave like that? You promised me."

Trickles of blood began to flow from my father's eyes and from the corners of his mouth.

An aunt came and dragged me away. She told me to calm down. She told me that even if someone is dead, the spirit is still in the body. "If you act like that," she said, "the spirit can't leave. The spirit is crying. He's crying blood. His life was hard enough. Just let him go, please, just let him go."

I watched with horror as the blood kept trickling. I went to his side and, as if comforting a child, said, "Please, it's okay, just go, I'm not blaming you, I know you tried your best. . . ."

I repeated it again and again, until I couldn't control my emotions and broke down wailing and sobbing.

The day after my father was cremated, he came to me in a dream. "I saw the offerings you burned," he said, angrily. "What am I going to do in the afterlife with that little car you offered me? Why not a motorcycle? I can't even drive a car."

When I woke up that morning, I told my mother about the dream. She had seen him, too, she said. He had told her to tell me to hurry up and get him a motorcycle. He wanted to take a ride up the coast.

"That sweet father of yours," my mother said, smiling.

# 4

# Christmas in the ICU

I remember the hallway that seemed to go on forever, with a marble floor that made even the softest footfalls echo long and loud. The sound of people coming and going in the hallway became a rumble. The chilly overhead lighting falling across the floor made it look even longer than it was.

The signs over each doorway down the long hallway stated the reason the people within had been gathered together: Cardiovascular, Neurosurgery. . . . Disease ruled that place, disease was the organizing principle, disease made the rules, and disease subsumed all other identities.

The people gathered together in those rooms—no matter who they were or what they had done, whether they had just stepped down from a dais or were dozing on the ridge between rice paddies—all woke up in the same place.

Wherever disease had found them, whatever lives they were living at the time, it had put them in the same place, confined together like farm animals.

They lay on the same white sheets, shielded by the same

white curtains, looking up at the same white ceiling. Their names were no longer important. What they had in common was disease. They might have never had reason to meet each other in another life, but there, relationships were reorganized by shared ailments, and two strangers could get to know each other intimately in a matter of days.

Most conversation was confined to topics corporeal. They would compare symptoms and sensations in great detail. Someone might say, "Today I can get four or five normal breaths before I have to take a deep breath. How about you?"

"I can get about six or seven."

"I started feeling a pain in my big toe today, on my left foot."

"Not me. But I can feel a sort of hot stream running down my . . ."

There's usually some distance or some separation between your consciousness and the vessel that carries it. But in that place they understood, perhaps for the first time, the clear barrier between body and soul. They learned to respect the body as much as they respected the soul or the emotions.

My father's illness is what brought me there. I was sixteen years old.

I am talking about the intensive care unit, the ICU. It was located on the top floor of the hospital. The elevator to the top floor opened on the long hallway hung with signs listing all those spine-chilling names. Each one of those diseases was given several rooms, as if it were territory captured by occupying forces and the patients within were prisoners of war. Before arriving at the ICU, I had no idea that hospitals operated on that kind of martial logic. The deadliest, most bloodthirsty diseases seized the high ground.

The outpatient department handled diseases too weak to hang on for long, and the morgue handled the bodies that disease had already abandoned. The still-thriving and the dead were set side by side.

That was because they were both the products of the most incompetent illnesses. Death is never disease's objective; the objective of disease is to occupy and then dominate the human body. Uncomplicated trauma or illness and death are both the result of disease executed without sophistication or elegance.

I often went through the outpatient department on my frequent trips to pick up supplies, or whenever I needed a break from the ICU.

There were two ways to get down from the top floor. The first option was an elevator right beside my father's room. That was the most direct route to the outpatient department, but the elevator was usually crowded. It stopped at each floor on the way down, providing a survey of each layer of disease: first the neuroscience ward, then internal medicine on the next floor, then surgery. . . . When the door opened onto the outpatient department, I was hit with a wave of spirited noise.

The second option was the staff elevator. It was always deserted. There was an unspoken rule that family members of ICU patients had free use of the elevator. The staff saw us as comrades-in-arms. We had a secret in common: we had both felt the breath of death on our necks.

The staff elevator was in the secluded southeast corner of the building, all the way at the end of the long hallway. The worst part of the trip was going from one end of the hallway to the other. I couldn't stop my eyes darting from doorway to doorway, checking each bed to see if anyone was missing. An unexpectedly empty bed would sometimes catch me by surprise.

I hated that feeling. It was like I was going along and had stepped in a crater in the road. My heart would sink.

That was the reason I usually took the main elevator to get down to the outpatient department. I knew I would have to go through the crowd of people, through the irritated chatter, through the humid fug of perspiration—but I liked submerging myself in it. Sometimes the noise of the outpatient department reminded me of a concert, and the thick smell of sweat gave me a peculiar sensation. Each time the elevator door opened, I knew I was in for a thrill, and I wondered what I would see and hear and smell. The joy of being human, I thought to myself.

Soon after arriving at the ICU, I found out that there were other kids among the families of the patients. I say that I found out about them because I never really got to know them.

There was an invisible barrier that kept any of us from becoming friends. Maybe it was something in their eyes. They seemed to be able to see right through me, right into my heart. Those were the eyes of someone who has experienced real pain; those were eyes that had been washed clear by tears. I knew because I had the same eyes.

It's painful to try to talk to someone with those penetrating eyes. You can't help but feel your chitchat is too vulgar or too simple, as if you are insulting them with your flimsy attempts at conversation. It felt like undergoing vivisection. It was better to steer clear of them and avoid a second attempt at a heart-to-heart.

We avoided each other by unspoken mutual agreement.

I think perhaps there was another reason. Since we were all children of patients, we already knew what lurked in each other's hearts. I knew what kind of pain they were in and how they put on a brave front. I knew how guilty they felt after trying to make a joke to forget everything they were going through.

So I didn't bother trying to make friends with anyone my own age.

After I came to that conclusion, whenever anyone tried to invade my space or get close to me, I would glare at them until they retreated.

But looking after my father wasn't enough to take my mind off the sorrow. In the ICU, if you give yourself a moment to ponder, your thoughts will overwhelm you. Those insidious emotions are the shameless mercenaries of disease.

There were all sorts of tiny tasks to take my mind off the situation. When I changed my father's IV, I had to search for a patch of skin not yet punctured by countless tiny holes. When the doctors had a new prescription for him, I had to choose between the "Made in China" option or the more expensive import. "Which one do you want?" the doctor asked. I asked the price of the import and thought for a long time.

"Will the 'Made in China' one have any extra side effects?"

"Probably. There might be some pain after administering it. There's no chance of that with the import."

I did a quick mental calculation of how much money we had left and how much longer my father might remain in the hospital. "I'll get the 'Made in China,'" I said.

Then I had to watch my father writhing in pain, unable to sleep.

The family of the patient in the room next to my father's used to scold me: "You need to look after him better than that. Don't try to skimp on his treatment!"

I could only laugh.

Early on, I decided I could make friends with ICU patients. There was no way I could make friends with their families—too sick with worry, too stressed out to be think-ing about friendship. The patients often had a sunny dispo-sition, even if it was nothing but a front. Perhaps the sun is the perfect comparison: to shine so bright, they had to burn what was inside of them for fuel.

I was drawn to a patient who stayed down the hall from my father's room. He was a dark, wiry man from Zhang-zhou, a city west of Xiamen, and old enough for me to call him uncle. He was confined to the ICU by heart disease. He often stopped to catch his breath while speaking, but other than that, he seemed fairly healthy.

He had been a healthy eater before, but he couldn't even eat a full bowl of rice by the time I met him. One day, chuckling, he told me the story of his first meeting with his wife and her family. He had gone for a meal, as custom dic-tated in this kind of marriage arrangement, and he shocked his future mother-in-law by wolfing down four heaping bowls of steamed rice. He figured it was because of that that she agreed to marry her daughter off to him. When I helped him to the bathroom, he would go into the stall by himself, then shake and shiver, waiting for something to come out. He would yell over the partition to me, "Can't even take a piss anymore, it just drips like a leaky pipe!"

He used to have fun with the nurses, maybe going over the line sometimes. If he saw one of them dressed up more than normal or wearing makeup, he would ask, "So, what time are you picking me up tonight?"

His relatives used to jokingly call him an old pervert.

That nickname became Ol' Bastard when it spread through the rest of the hospital.

"Tell us a joke, Ol' Bastard," someone said.

He was eating an apple.

"Did we lose you, Ol' Bastard?"

He laughed and said, "I'm still here, I'm still here, I'm not dead yet."

My father was jealous of our friendship. He wanted to joke around with me, too. He tried to entice me with stories about his younger years, about old girlfriends or scams he had run with his gang. But I still went to visit the man from Zhangzhou. I used to tell my father to take him as an example: "Just look at him, he's still got happiness down in his heart. That's better than any medicine."

My father abandoned the rivalry, but he refused to ever talk to him.

I took a trip each evening down to the second-floor cafeteria and picked up the same items I always did: three portions of rice porridge, a portion of meat, a portion of vegetables, and—with my usual second-guessing whether I should—a bit of braised pork for the man from Zhangzhou. His doctor had told him to stay away from the fatty, sweet glazed belly meat, and his family would never buy it for him, but I always grabbed a portion to secretly slip to him.

Each night, I got off the elevator and stopped to see him first before going to my father's room.

But one evening, returning from the cafeteria, I found his bed empty. I thought for a moment and decided that his family must have taken him out for dinner. I took the food to my father's room and we started to eat. "That guy from Zhangzhou, he's not in his room," I casually said. "Did his family take him out? If they were celebrating something, they should have invited me along."

"He passed away," my mother said flatly, not looking at me.

I wordlessly finished eating, then went up to the roof of the hospital to watch the sun go down. I vowed never to make friends with an ICU patient again. I sneaked back into my father's room, pulled out the recliner chair, and lay down. I pretended I wasn't sad.

Auntie Wang was one of the most popular people on the ward. She was one of the cleaning women, and like the rest of them, she carried the smell of the soil with her. She had a powerful voice and was a hard worker.

Thinking back, though, she wasn't really a good person. If there was nothing in it for her, she wasn't interested. If she didn't pretend to forget her task, she would still help you out, but she would be grumbling the entire time, cursing you under her breath. Her way of speaking was not particularly pleasant. Sometimes the children of patients who had just arrived would play in the hallway, getting in her way, and she would fling her mop aside and roar, "Who do these kids belong to? Brats! We've got people dying here and they're running around having fun!"

Their cries would echo down the hallway, then an adult would sneak in like a thief and spirit them away. The next sound you would hear was faint sobbing from a room on the ward.

The only reason she managed to get along with anyone is because the ICU was a sort of exclusive community. She also had the least contact with disease. There was no need to worry about certain things around her. There was no need to cover up your grief. There was no chance that she would suddenly disappear from the ward. And her bad temper also had its advantages: there was no expectation or reason to form any permanent relationship with her.

I saw many families leave and never come back. Once they had the chance to leave, they seemed to wipe from their memories any traces of the place. It was as if the ICU was a parallel universe.

I tried to sympathize with Auntie Wang. Like me, she must have formed some relationships with patients—and then those new friends disappeared. She learned how to shield herself. She knew that the families of the ICU, as genuine as they might have seemed, would one day leave and never return.

I felt a new warmth toward her when I realized what she must have been through.

I tried to figure out what made Auntie Wang happy. She definitely liked to gossip. She told the story of Old Wang in the fourth-floor orthopedics department, who tottered over to the toilet with a broken leg, then wound up slipping and breaking his other leg. She described both his legs suspended over the bed like a big V. But her biggest contribution to hospital gossip was the story of conjoined twins born to a mother in the maternity ward of the obstetrics department on the second floor. The parents were sobbing, she told us, and the doctors were still trying to figure out how to separate them. "I went and got a look at them," Auntie Wang said, "while I was cleaning down there. They look like a pair of temple gods!" She became animated when relating juicy gossip, speaking with her hands.

I could not stop thinking about the twins. For several days, the entire ICU seemed to be discussing it. Everyone tried to picture how they would live.

It was like a soap opera for us, with each new twist and turn in the series related to us by Auntie Wang. She arrived one morning and announced that the conjoined twins were two baby boys. "What a shame it turned out like this," someone said. "Twin boys are such a blessing."

She returned later that same day to break the news that the doctors planned to use a surgical saw to separate the twins. It was just a matter of time, she told us. The ICU was in an uproar, with everyone speculating about the procedure. The patients of the ICU had undergone their fair share of surgeries, so they had their own theories about how it might be done.

The next day, everyone was waiting for the next installment. Auntie Wang did not disappoint. "They have only one heart," she said.

Everyone came together to discuss the update. "*Ai-ya!*
That means they're going to be stuck together for the rest
of their lives," someone said, "eat together, sleep together,
forever."

The obstetrics department, which included the maternity ward, was on the same floor as the cafeteria, so every
time I finished picking up food, I would sneak over for a
look. I was free to roam the hospital, since all of the nurses
knew me and would usually wave me in to stroll around
other parts of the hospital, but that privilege, accorded to
family members of ICU patients, did not extend to the
obstetrics department. They knew we were in close prox-
imity to death, and they didn't want to risk us passing it on
to the hospital's newest arrivals.

Gossip from the maternity ward was the most highly
prized. Everyone would hang on every word of a story
about a newborn. The maternity ward was like some fan-
tastic tourist site. The ICU children were always looking
for ways to sneak in.

Various ruses were employed, like pretending to be
dropping off food or saying they had to pick up a prescription there, or even using a doctor's cap and a surgical mask
as a disguise. They all failed.

I finally convinced Auntie Wang to take me with her to
the maternity ward in exchange for a set of tutoring books
she planned to give to her own kids.

I was given a mop bucket to carry, and Auntie Wang
told me to follow her in the ward. She panted as she

walked, and I could smell her body odor. Two nurses on duty watched the door to the ward like soldiers at a road-block. They looked at me skeptically.

"I'm not feeling good today," Auntie Wang said by way of explanation, "so he offered to help me out. He's a good boy."

The nurses conferred, then handed me a blue nurse's jacket to wear. But as I followed Auntie Wang into the ward, one of the nurses called me back. "You need to go to the disinfection room and get clean first!"

I knew what the nurse was thinking. I threw down the jacket and ran back to the ICU.

I had given up on trying to see the conjoined twins. Auntie Wang kept updating us, though, until about a week after my foiled maternity ward visit, when she dropped the topic completely. Nobody could get anything out of her.

Everyone realized what had happened. It was the same thing that they were all dreading could happen to them or their loved one.

That which could not be named had stolen in and carried the twins away. It might come for them next.


When I saw the way they looked at each other, I knew exactly what was going on between the head nurse and the new doctor.

When she was a younger woman, the head nurse must have been a pretty young thing. Her face had kept its elegant shape at least. There were two dimples in her cheeks that deepened when she smiled, but as long as I had known her, she usually wore a cold expression and spoke in a dull monotone.

There was a nurses' station in the middle of the ICU. It had a counter like you might find in a nightclub, about waist height, and it was located right beside what we called the VIP room. The door to the VIP room was always closed. Doctors could come and go as they pleased, but patients needed an invitation.

Nobody was quite sure what the interior of the room looked like, so it became a topic of speculation in the ICU. Rumor had it that there were European-style furnishings and a shag rug, and some said there was even a pool table.

However, we all knew that one day we would receive the call. An invitation to the VIP room meant that your family member was at the crossroads of life and death. The meeting in the VIP room was about the final surgical option.

The procedure began like this: the afternoon before the surgery was scheduled, the head nurse would arrive with a smile and a notification form for the patient's family. "The doctors want to have a word with you tonight," she would say. "Bring whomever you want to accompany you." At eight o'clock, the head nurse would tap at the door and lead the family into the VIP room.

The door to the VIP room would open briefly and

then swing shut as the family entered. The next morning, the patient whose family had received the VIP invitation would be sent to the operating room. That was the last anybody saw of them. If the surgery was successful, the patient would be transferred to a recovery room for observation before either being sent to one of the wards on the lower floors or discharged directly. If the surgery was a failure, return to the ICU was unnecessary.

The romance between the head nurse and the young doctor had everyone in the ICU on pins and needles. In a place like that, love was usually an extreme thing, either unimaginable joy or crushing sorrow. The patients had practical concerns, too, since a change in the head nurse's mood might mean that she would be careless when giving the next injection. Everyone in the ICU studied their faces for the slightest changes in emotion, but the head nurse and the doctor never dropped the mask of professionalism.

It was even more stressful for me because the doctor was in charge of vascular conditions, so when it was time for surgery, he might hold my father's life in his hands.

The romance between the nurse and the young doctor became a matter of public safety. There was constant whispered speculation about the progress of their relationship and discussion of how things might be pushed forward.

The first reaction had been to find a way to drive them apart. There were suggestions that we should start a rumor to break them up. When the head nurse came around to give an injection, a patient would drop a story that they had seen the doctor hanging around a nurse from a lower floor. "Oh?" the head nurse would say. "Is that so?" She might have appeared calm, but the way she jabbed the needle in gave her away—and it left the poor patient moaning in pain.

Another patient took it into his head that he should introduce the young doctor to another eligible bachelorette, promising him that she was prettier than the head nurse and from a wealthy family. When the head nurse got word of the scheme, she stormed into his room. "I think you're enjoying your time in here a little too much," she said, arms crossed across her chest.

After that, everyone decided it was preferable to have the courtship proceed with as much stability as possible. Family members of patients would hang around trying to overhear the head nurse, then it would be passed on to someone else, who would go to the young doctor to drop hints. If the head nurse seemed upset, we would do our best to get out of her whatever the issue might be, then do our best to make it right.

My role in the project was minimal. I was charged with complimenting the head nurse whenever I saw her—"You look beautiful today"—and observing to the young doctor how considerate and responsible the head nurse was. "You know," I would say to him, "that's the type of woman I'd like to marry."

I always seemed to run into the doctor in the bathroom, though. He would take his time zipping up his pants, then turn to me and let me have it. "You little bastard," he said, "don't let me hear you going around talking like that again or I'll give you a cuff upside the head." I nodded. I couldn't reveal that I was only playing my part in the scheme. The next time I saw him, I repeated it again.

We struggled through each day as best we could, but at least we found things like that to entertain us temporarily. Things seemed to be getting better with my father's condition, too. That might mean he was well enough to attempt surgery. Doctors started prescribing milder medications. I got the sense that our visit to the VIP room was imminent.

I was right. It wasn't long before the call came. The head nurse led my mother and me behind the counter of the nurses' station and into the VIP room. There were several large desks with office chairs, and then a big, soft sofa, which sat like a plush oasis in one corner of the room.

The sofa was meant for the family to sit on. It was supposed to make them feel safe and comfortable.

I didn't have time to process the disappointment at the lack of a shag rug or a pool table. The doctor in charge of my father's treatment was waiting on one side of the sofa. He smiled as we entered, rose to greet us, and gave me a surprisingly firm handshake. I realized that all of this—the smile, the sofa, the firmness of the handshake—must have been the product of careful research into the best way to handle the family of patients ahead of surgery.

A few other doctors took their places around the room, and I noticed the young doctor was among them. I had guessed right: he was going to be involved in my father's surgery.

The head doctor launched into a detailed explanation of the surgery that completely baffled me and my mother.

My mother cut him off. "Doctor, I just want to know what his chances are."

"I give him a 60 percent chance. I want you to know what the risks are. During the surgery, his heart will be temporarily replaced by an artificial heart. If his blood pressure drops too low while he's hooked to the machine, it might be impossible to save him. But if we can stabilize him and perform the surgery, our plan is to replace the valve with an artificial valve. The risk with that is an air bubble in his circulation. If that's the case, then again, it might be impossible to save him."

My mother looked like she was about to faint. She motioned for the head doctor to stop.

"I'm sorry," he said, "but this is necessary. It's my duty to inform you of the risks."

The head doctor's lecture seemed to take an eternity. "Can we get your consent to perform the surgery?" he asked finally. "I've told you that I can predict a 60 percent success rate for the surgery, but you need to weigh that against his prospects without surgery. If that valve is not replaced, it's not likely he'll live to see next spring."

My mother was speechless. She turned to me. "I want you to decide," she said. "You're the head of the family now."

"Can I think on it?" I asked.

"That's fine," the head doctor said, "but time is limited. We need to do the surgery before it's too late. We have a window of opportunity here and now. We want to schedule him for the morning of the day after tomorrow."

When I left the VIP room, I went by myself to the roof of the hospital. I noticed for the first time the ring of chain-link fence around its edge. Maybe it was there for when people had abandoned hope.

I expected to be alone up on the roof, but I saw that another boy about my age was there, too. I recognized him. I had seen him leaving the VIP room shortly before my mother and I went in. I guessed that the same responsibility had been thrust upon him.

The unspoken rules of the ICU dictated that we should ignore each other, but he unexpectedly broke the silence. "Did you know tomorrow is Christmas?"

"Is that right?" I said. I hadn't realized.

"My father wanted to be back home by Spring Festival. He said he wanted to see the fireworks. Can you set off fireworks on Christmas?"

"I don't think so."

We both turned to look at the falling darkness, then

down at the city below, with its crowded streets and its tapestry of lights coming to life in the dusk.

I signed the consent form. I went back to the VIP room alone because my mother was afraid she would start shaking if she had to face the doctors and desks again.

When I had finished, the young doctor was put in charge of preparing me. "Tomorrow night," he said, "I want you to make sure he's mentally prepared to go into surgery. That means taking care of anything he might ask for. He has to want to survive this. If someone wants to live, if they're really holding on to this world, their chances of making it through go up. But you need to make sure he's ready."

As usual, I was in charge of fetching dinner that night. My mother wanted to get my father his favorite marinated duck. He couldn't eat it, but she thought it might be nice if he could look at it. But I suddenly had another idea. I went and bought him his least favorite food: fish slices and greens.

My father was upset and nagged me all night.

I tried to comfort him. "The day after tomorrow," I said, "I'll buy you something—how about a whole duck?"

My father had no idea that the surgery had a 60 percent success rate, but he knew enough to be anxious. He seemed to want to impart some final wisdom to me. "I want you to look after your mother," he said.

"I'm not ready to look after her. I'm too young."

That did nothing to settle his nerves.

He paused and took a deep breath. "Why aren't your uncles here?" he asked. "I should call them. I have a few things I need to tell them."

"They have their own problems to deal with. They don't have time to talk to you. Just wait until you get out of here. You can talk to them then."

He glared at me. "You know you're not supposed to upset a sick person, right?"

"I'm not trying to upset you," I said. "I'm telling you the truth. They said they'd come over the day after tomorrow. They can spend the whole day with you."

"You're tricky, aren't you?" he said, then he went quiet.

The surgery was a gamble, and I didn't know if it was worth taking. If my father didn't make it, I knew I would regret that conversation for the rest of my life.

I heard a child out in the hallway shouting about Christmas. He was asking someone for a present, but I didn't hear anyone react. The child's cries were like a stone dropped into a well too deep to hear a splash. He did not know what I knew. There were days far more important than Christmas Day.

My mother could not take it. She was depressed and anxious. She went to open the window to get some fresh air. At that very moment, a streak of light rocketed up from the ground, cutting through the murky darkness, climbing up and up until it was almost level with the window. When it reached its apex, it blossomed into a bright, multicolored ball of light: someone was setting off fireworks.

That made everyone on the ICU happy: "Fireworks!"

The lights from the colorful explosion flashed. I turned and saw that my father was smiling. How wonderful, fireworks.

I immediately knew who had lit the fuse down below. I realized how much he must love his father. I stuck my head out the window and saw the boy from the rooftop with three security guards surrounding him.

At nine o'clock on the day of his surgery, my father was wheeled into the operating room. My uncles and the rest of the cousins had arrived the night before. We stood outside the door.

There were a few chairs outside the operating room, but they were cheap plastic stools like the kind you would find at a cheap restaurant. Nobody could sit on one for very long before deciding it was better to stand.

Around ten o'clock, a nurse rushed out of the room. My mother broke down in tears. Nobody dared ask the nurse what was going on.

A short time after that, a team of doctors walked by us and went into the operating room. Ignoring hospital regulations, my uncles took out cigarettes and lit up.

At twelve o'clock, there was still no news from the operating room. The nurses and doctors had stopped coming and going. Everyone in the waiting room stewed in anxiety.

The silence was so complete that we could hear the second hand of the clock moving. A few of the relatives wanted to find someone to ask how the surgery was going, but the door to the operating room was shut tight. Nobody was coming or going.

A little after one o'clock, a lone nurse stepped out of the operating room and brushed past us without saying a word.

Some of the family started to cry.

My uncles had had enough. "What are you crying for?" one of them asked.

"They're busy in there," the other one said. "You're all imagining the worst." The two men threw their cigarette butts to the floor and went to stand in the corner.

When my father was finally wheeled out of surgery and into the recovery room, I looked around for the boy who had set off the fireworks, but he was nowhere to be found.

"Did you get any other patients out of surgery today?" I asked a nurse.

"Just your father," the nurse said.

I couldn't sit still. I sneaked off without telling anyone and went back up to the ICU. The patients and their families couldn't hide their excitement. But I wasn't in the mood for their congratulations.

"Do you know the patient who had surgery on the same day as my father?" I asked. "How is he?"

Someone seemed to know whom I meant.

"Right, that must be who it was," I said. "He has a boy about the same age as me."

"He went in for surgery yesterday. We never saw him come out," someone finally explained.

I turned and walked to the elevator without speaking. I rode it down to the first floor and walked out through the outpatient department. The marks of the fireworks were still on the pavement outside. There was not much left, just a layer of gray ash.

I knew that in a few days the wind would blow it away, and the dust of the city would bury all traces.

Not much left. As if it never happened at all.

# 5

# Friends in High Places

It was not long after my father's funeral that he began to appear in my mother's dreams. The man she saw was still partially paralyzed, as my father had been in his final years. In the dream, she glimpsed him across a creek. He was squatting there, leaning to one side, smiling slightly, looking at her peacefully.

Nothing in particular seemed to happen in these dreams. They were quite tranquil in fact. But she was not prepared to chalk them up to simple grief. This was her conclusion: "Your father is coming to me for help."

"There must be something from this life still hanging over him," she told me, "some debt he couldn't repay. That's why he still looks like he did after his stroke. If someone's soul has moved on, they can't keep appearing in your dreams. They appear one final time, and then they disappear."

There were two things my mother was sure of: the first was that "we all have debts to pay in this life, and you can't leave this world until you pay them," and the second was that "if someone's soul has moved on, they can't keep appearing in your dreams."

My mother made a solemn promise to help my father.

Only much later I learned that when my mother was young, she was a hard-boiled skeptic. She didn't believe in anything supernatural. That was surprising, since her mother had been a sort of shaman.

My mother was born shortly after the founding of New China. That was in 1949, a time when the political was paramount and slogans went up in the ancestral shrines and temples. My grandmother and nana kept belief alive, and they never stopped offering incense to the gods and ancestors. In fact, my mother's skepticism had nothing to do with politics. Times were hard, and she was hungry; she didn't believe her family could be abandoned to their fate like this if there really were gods.

My mother had three sisters, one older than her and two younger, and two brothers, one older and one younger. That large family was the result of a campaign to increase the birth rate. The same as everywhere else in this world, the government was mostly concerned with the theoretical—how to increase the number of children being born—but the quotidian aspects of the campaign (feeding all of those children, for example) were sometimes too minor to fall within the scope of their concerns. The person in charge of feeding the children was my grandmother, who was, like my father, partially paralyzed. She worked as a shaman at home. My mother was happy to talk about that time in her life, but she always avoided exaggerating what she had gone through. As she told it, they had to get through it one way or another. She went through the same things as everyone else, she said. Her suffering was not unique; what was unique were the ways different people invented to deal with it.

In our Hokkien culture, women and girls are supposed to be virtuous and dutiful, but my mother learned to be tough. She was the first girl to climb up into a tree to pick fruit. The fruit was a help, but it wasn't much, so she shocked her family by becoming an expert at trapping crabs and netting shrimp. She was good at it because she took risks. She got up at four or five every morning, long before anybody else was up, and went down into the marshes. She was willing to go places where nobody else would (the waters around the rocky atoll were teeming with marine life, but most people wouldn't take the risk, since it was impossible to approach by boat without running aground, and if you went on foot, you ran the risk of being caught in a tidal current). . . . My mother nearly didn't make it back from one such expedition.

The bigger the risk, the richer the reward: it's a rule that applies to many things in this world. Dusk was the best time to fish the atoll, but it was also the most dangerous time, when the tide was sweeping back in to submerge it. The currents were fierce and carried a legion of waves that crashed against the atoll. Anyone unlucky enough to be caught on the rocky outcropping at that time faced the waves and tidal currents but also the inexorable rise of the ocean around them.

One evening, my mother's hunger and greed kept her at the atoll past the point when she could safely escape the tide. The water was rising all around her. The waves came, trying to take her in their embrace. The ocean rose, threatening to swallow her. There was a small boat not too far away, and someone on board had seen what was happening. They tried to get close enough to rescue her, but the waves tossed the boat around, and the pilot was finally forced to retreat. The people on the boat could only yell to her from across the water.

My mother was forced to rescue herself. She gritted her teeth, slung the afternoon's catch over her shoulder, took a deep breath, and jumped into the sea. There was something childish in her resolve, like a toddler throwing a tantrum. The waves tore at her, but perhaps because she refused to give in, the demons of the sea tossed her back. She was spun out of the labyrinthine currents and spit into the open ocean, with her catch still over her shoulder.

According to her, when she was pulled into the boat, she kept her head held high. She didn't let on how frightened she was. But that was her last trip to fish the atoll. "I still remember how alone I felt," she told me. "I can still feel it."

For many years after I heard the story, I tried to imagine my mother diving in to battle the currents. She had the arrogance of youth, when you are completely unafraid because you are ignorant of the dangers you face. She relied on some instinct, some innate sense, to struggle through the chaos of the waves. Whatever fate held in store for her, my mother went in the opposite direction.

She told me that my grandmother, from the time my

mother was a girl, used to sigh and say, "How is a tomboy like you ever going to raise a child or be a good wife?"

When gods want to bring a mortal to their side, they discover what a person's life is lacking and then bestow it. Most people do not know what it is they really want or need; in fact, my mother told me, they're afraid of discovering what it might be.

Even during those revolutionary years, the Hokkien people clung to their customs. These customs, even if outmoded, were passed on in a self-perpetuating cycle.

My mother, like all the women of southern Fujian, was obligated, beginning in her teenage years, to take part in the arranged dates that would lead to her finding a husband. At that young age, her future life, and the man who would play a central role in it, was glimpsed as a blur, like something vastly remote. My mother and her peers knew the steps required to fulfill their womanhood: the first step was to get married; the second was to bear a son for their husband, so that another entry could be recorded in the family genealogy and the family name passed on to another generation; the third was to make enough money to look after their children; the fourth was to save up for a daughter's dowry (if the dowry was too meager, bullying could be expected from their future in-laws); the fifth was to pay the bride-price and hold a wedding for their son; the sixth was to ensure that a grandson was born and the family name would be passed on again; the seventh was to help raise that grandson; and once all of those steps were complete, matriarchal responsibility was passed on to the next generation along with all the customs and traditions, and the women of the last generation were relegated to a supervisory role. When the gods and ancestors had deemed a woman's work complete, she would finally be summoned out of this world and on to her next life.

For women like my mother, each step of their adult lives was laid out for them, slowly leading them toward a "happily ever after." When my father and his parents visited my mother's family, my mother stood in the corner, giving my father a brief glimpse and an almost imperceptible nod. The slight nod was her giving her assent to a firm push toward adulthood.

The first major test came when her first child was a daughter. The family offered their best wishes, but she knew that their kind words tactfully concealed an exhortation to make sure that her second child was a son. The pressure came not only from the family—my mother dearly wanted a son, too. She wanted a son to inherit her impulsiveness and stubbornness.

The second test was coming, and my mother managed to maintain her composure for most of her pregnancy, but she cracked a month before she went into labor. She broke down crying and went to the Lady of Linshui temple and vowed to its goddess of motherhood that if she gave birth to a son, she would stop denying the supernatural and pledge her eternal belief in the gods.

I was born a month later.

My mother described how she had wound up at that particular temple. In southern Fujian, unlike most of China, temples are not segregated by sect. Inside a large temple, there are often gods and deities from numerous faiths, so you might find the Three Buddhas beside a shrine to the Daoist deity Guan Yu, and then an altar to local earth gods beside a temple to Mazu, the goddess of the sea.

When she first arrived at the temple, she had no idea exactly how to go about petitioning the gods for assistance or which gods in particular would be the most effective. Finally, an elderly woman passed by and explained to her that the gods each have their own jurisdiction and constituents: there is a kitchen god for the kitchen, there are earth gods for agricultural concerns, and each village or district has its own local deities. "Whatever you're going through, you can find a god who can talk you through it or take some of the burden off you." At that moment, my mother wanted to believe.

"I realized that whatever I was carrying with me was going to crush me," my mother told me, "and I thought it sounded great, the idea that there was a god who could take some of the weight off me."

I'm not sure how many people in our hometown have quite the same relationship to the gods as my mother does. From as far back as I can remember, she treated the gods with the casualness of family, dropping by the temple like she would drop by a cousin's place. Whenever anything was bothering her, the first place she would go was a temple.

To talk to the gods, she used her moon blocks. These

were two blocks of wood, both flat on one side and curved on the other. She would ask a question and then divine the answer by tossing the wooden crescents to the floor. The answer was contained in the various positions the blocks took after coming to rest. The three possible answers were yes, no, or no comment. She poured out her complaints to the gods, whispered a possible solution to the moon blocks, then cast them to get the response. She could weep and wail to the god in his niche but then turn to me with a smile on her face.

She often treated the gods like a spoiled child might treat doting parents. When she got a negative response from her moon blocks, she would throw them again and again until she got the answer she wanted. Once she was satisfied, she would smile guilelessly up at the god, who was at that very moment cruising through the heavens on a towering cumulonimbus, and say, "Thanks!"

I didn't really understand what my mother was going through that drove her to seek solace in those temples. What I remember is the thick scent of agarwood climbing slowly upward and the clatter of moon blocks on floorboards.

It was my mother's idea for me to be adopted by a god. I was around three or four years old when my divine godfather was introduced to me. Around the time she was pregnant with me, things at home had been rough, and maybe because of that, I was born a sickly child. The way I heard it, my mother had gone to the Guan Yu shrine in the old city and thrown her moon blocks until she got the answer she wanted. After receiving the blessing of Guan Yu, we went to the shrine each year, carrying offerings of pork knuckle. The temple attendant would give me incense and joss paper to burn, securing another year's blessing.

I didn't understand exactly what function this divine godfather played in my life or how he could bestow protection on me, but I began to feel at home in those temples, like I was stopping by to visit relatives. Visitors to the Guan Yu shrine could pull strips of lottery poetry to have their fortunes told. The poems on the strips of paper were fables written in the style of classical poetry, and I would take the lottery poetry strips home with me and read them before bed. It was almost like my godfather was tucking me in with a bedtime story.

According to local custom, my divine godfather only held his title until I turned sixteen. After that, I was an adult and no longer under his fatherly protection. But I couldn't break the habit of going to see my godfather at least once a year to say a prayer and make offerings. Whenever life got me down, I would visit Guan Yu and spend an afternoon talking to him with a set of moon blocks.

When my father had the stroke that left him partially paralyzed, my mother's first reaction was to march angrily over to the temple and demand answers from the gods.

There was not really much in the way of a conversation between my mother and the gods. My mother provided the answers to her own questions, then used the moon blocks to confirm. My mother came up with her own solutions to her problems, so even if the gods did intervene, they were simply helping her choose from among her own suggestions.

The answer my mother confirmed with the gods after my father's stroke was this: it was his fate, and it was her fate to stay by his side and help him.

I knew that was the answer she wanted to receive. Deep down, she was still the stubborn, fearless girl who had jumped into the waves.

Even though the doctor's assessment had been that there was almost no chance he would ever regain full use of the left side of his body, my mother refused to give up. My parents put together a three-year plan to nurse him back to health. But unfortunately, the doctor's assessment was correct, and my father's condition deteriorated until he struggled to get out of bed.

In the years after my father's stroke, my mother dragged me along with her to make an annual trip to each temple, throwing her moon blocks and insisting on a prophecy from each god about my father's chances for recovery that year. A year later, she would go back to demand why they hadn't lived up to their promises.

My father's left side slowly withered, but the rest of his body seemed to swell. Four years after the stroke, he was so large that when he fell, my mother could no longer help him up.

My mother would rush off to the temples to desperately demand an explanation for why my father wasn't recovering. She went again and again, even though we still went on our usual year-end trip to worship at the temples.

One year on the fateful day, she didn't throw her moon blocks as she normally did, but instead lit incense and pulled me over to kneel before the altar before starting a mumbling prayer.

At first, I couldn't hear what she was saying, but I finally pieced together enough fragments and realized with sudden horror what she was praying for: "Please take my husband before me. Please don't let him be a burden on the children. I know it's fate, but please lend me a few more years, at least so I can live longer than my husband. I can die after I see him off."

I wheeled on her and demanded to know what she was thinking. She slapped me, then went quiet for a long time. When she broke the silence, she said, "I'm doing this for you."

I knelt down at the altar and made my own childish request: "Please let me and my father and my mother all go at the same time."

When my mother heard me, she came over and hit me again, then wailed to the gods, "He's too young to know what he's saying! Listen to me!"

On our way home from the temple that day, my mother turned to me solemnly and began to lay out how she saw the future playing out: "All you need to worry about is school. Get into a good university, make your own money, get married, live your own life. Your father is my responsibility. I will live as long as he does. I will take care of everything."

"But you can't even lift him when he falls," I said.

"I'll be fine."

"But how are you going to cover all of his expenses? You're not getting any younger. Things aren't going to get any better."

"I'll be fine."

"But what about looking after yourself? What happens if you're not well enough to look after him?"

My mother rolled her eyes at me. "I'll be fine," she repeated impatiently.

"But you're my parents!"

My mother stopped walking. "You listen to me," she said firmly. "It's fate. I was meant to stand beside him. This is between him and me. It has nothing to do with you." She paused, and then added, "That's what the gods told me."


I knew better than to tell my father about my mother's grim prayer.

With any hope of recovery becoming faint, my father turned to the gods himself, grumbling to the deities and ancestors on our household altar, "If you aren't going to let me get well, then let me die." That always caused my mother to lose her temper.

"Don't talk like that!" she would say. "It's up to fate.

Don't complain to them about it. You'll go when it's time to go. Don't sit there complaining!"

Even though my father was often confined to his bed, he looked healthier than he had in years. His cheeks even took on a rosy hue. "He's like my big baby," she would say proudly to whoever would listen. "Even if he can't get around, he might just end up living to eighty."

Although I remained skeptical, I was happy enough to go along with my mother's judgment. The difficulty of looking after my father increased as his body bloated and his left side withered, but I knew she would continue to look after him. She would keep up the good fight to the very end. In her heart of hearts, she believed it was her fate to look after her husband.

One winter day, my father departed this world. Just as my mother had prayed, he went before her.

But my mother could not accept it. Although his left side had steadily lost feeling, she had seen his right side getting stronger. He had to support himself with his strong side, so his right hand and right foot were surprisingly muscular. "I don't understand how one fall could do it," she said. "I saw him fall a thousand times. He didn't even have any bruises. How could it happen just like that?"

I dropped what I was doing in Beijing and rushed home. When I got there, she was still looking for some explanation. She was just about to head out when I walked in the door. She wanted to go from temple to temple demanding an explanation from the gods. I hurried over and blocked her way. She fell into my arms crying. "Maybe they didn't understand me," she said. "I didn't think looking after him was a burden. When I made that prayer, all I meant was that I didn't want him to be a burden on you. I would have looked after him until I was a hundred years old!"

"They didn't make a mistake," I said. "Maybe it was just his fate to go. He lived a hard life, but he must have finally atoned for all of his sins."

My mother gaped at me. She thought for a moment and said, "Well, I guess you're right. He was in pain for so many years, but he's in a better place now. Let him enjoy it."

But the day after my father's funeral, my mother started to see him in her dreams. "Your father must be in trouble," she told me.

"That's not it," I said. "He just misses you. He wanted to check on you."

"No, I have to help him."

"How are you going to help him? You don't even know what his problem is."

"I'll figure it out," she said seriously.

If you want to find out what's happening down below, you have to find a shaman.

Once you find a shaman, you can have them lend their body for the spirit of the deceased to speak through. This is called spirit-seeking.

Where I come from, being a shaman is not a particularly unusual occupation. It is no more outlandish to call yourself a shaman than it is to call yourself a doctor or a fisherman. When the topic of shamans came up, nobody betrayed the slightest hint of skepticism. Asking about a shaman was no different than asking for a recommendation of a stonemason. There was the same discussion of credentials and skills.

My mother went in search of a shaman and came up with several possibilities. She heard about one on the west side of town who was especially good at making contact with those who had been deceased for many years. There was one up north, a village witch, who didn't need to wait for the relatives to say anything but could immediately channel the deceased and have them introduce themselves and start recalling stories from the past, but everything was communicated in the form of opera. And there was another on the east side who required that the family members directly request the deceased and provide some details, but the shaman would press the spirit to recollect some memories as proof of identity, and the spirits spoke in their own voices rather than arias.

After weighing all the pros and cons, my mother decided to go with the north side shaman.

Shamanism might have been a regular profession in our hometown, but you had to be careful choosing one.

The shaman's job was to peer into the crack between worlds and locate the soul of the deceased, so there was considerable risk involved. Offending a supernatural being or becoming entangled with spirits could bring a great deal of trouble.

My mother was hesitant when I asked to accompany her to see the shaman. She had heard that it was easier to contact a spirit if more family members were present, but there was also a superstition that the supernatural beings inhabiting the netherworld were easily attracted by the strong life force of younger people, so it might be risky for me to be there when we made contact, and my mother didn't want me getting involved.

When my mother told me why she was hesitant, my curiosity only increased. "Why don't you pray to your friends over at the temple for some help?" I suggested. "Maybe they can give me some paper charms or something."

My mother thought it was a great idea. She spent the afternoon touring temples and came back with a dozen protective amulets and a bag of incense ash.

My mother told me that not many of the gods agreed with her spirit-seeking to contact my father. Their reasoning, my mother suggested, was that life and death are decided by fate. We all have karmic debts to pay off in this life, and that's up to fate, too. If we fail to pay off those debts, we move on to the afterlife to continue working at clearing the slate. Before the day comes when those debts have been paid off, there's not much gods can do to intervene. "But then I asked them, what's the point of doing good deeds in this life if it's fine to leave our karmic debts to our afterlife? We do good deeds to atone for our sins in this life, right? Your father's on his way to the next life, but there's no reason he can't try to clear those debts before he gets there." I knew how my mother was. She refused to take no for an answer, even from the gods.

"The gods agreed to bless our efforts," she said, satisfied.

My mother offered a stick of incense and mumbled what city and neighborhood she was from and whom she was looking for.

I offered another stick of incense and said when he had died and how old he was.

We kowtowed three times.

After we finished the preliminaries, the shaman's assistant invited us to wait in the courtyard.

The shaman lived in a traditional home with two rows of brick buildings separated by a courtyard. It seemed that the shaman's family had once been wealthy and powerful. As for why their descendant had become a shaman or why they seemed to have moved out en masse, there was no way for me to know.

The shaman was stationed in the main room of the innermost house. There was a large altar, but it was impossible to tell what gods or idols were being worshipped, since the shaman, unlike most Hokkien people, had hung a yellow cloth in front of the shrine.

Anyone arriving to make a request of a shaman needs to offer incense to the gods of the shaman's shrine first, tell them what the purpose of the visit is, then kowtow three times. After that process is complete, the visitor is led to the second courtyard. When we arrived at the courtyard, the wooden door was closed behind us. The door seemed to be made of good wood. It was very heavy, and its lines true. It felt as if we were being locked out of our own world.

We shared the courtyard with many other people who had come to request the shaman's help. Some of them were pacing anxiously, trying to listen to what was going on inside the house, but most of them seemed too exhausted to move.

From time to time, the sound of the shaman singing came from inside the house. "I am from such and such district," he chanted, "such and such village. . . ." Then the shaman, in the voice of the deceased spirit, would announce a time of death and begin listing relatives who might be waiting to meet them.

When the shaman found a match, the relatives in the courtyard would begin to wail, saying, "Yes, your brother is here," or "Yes, your wife is here to see you!"

The sound of chanting mixed with sobbing and wailing.

When we arrived, the shaman's assistant had told us, "There is no guarantee that he will be able to contact the spirit of your loved one. He has so many spirits coming to see him. If you hear your loved one speak through the shaman, you can answer back. But if there is no contact, you'll have to make another appointment and come back."

As soon as I had a chance to sit for a moment and observe the spectacle, I started to have suspicions. This shaman probably sends someone out to pick up the obituaries and fish for information, I thought to myself. When the relatives arrive, he can randomly call out details in the voice of the departed spirit.

I was just about to break the news to my mother when the sound of chanting came again: "I hope my relatives from Xizhai are waiting for me. I'm on my way, leaning on my cane."

As soon as she heard "cane," my mother let out a gasp and dragged me into the house.

The windows of the room had been completely blacked out, the only light coming from a dim lamp. The smell of agarwood filled the air. The shaman limped toward us. I still had my doubts, but I couldn't deny that his bent back and shambling walk looked a lot like my father's.

"My son," the shaman said, "I am sorry. I am worried about you." I couldn't contain the flood of emotion that burst forth. I broke down in tears.

The shaman began to chant, letting my father speak through him. He said that he was not willing to leave, that he knew he had been a burden in the years after the stroke left him paralyzed, that he was thankful for my mother's care, that he was worried about my future. After those lamentations, my father—speaking through the shaman—began to make his predictions: "My son was born under a scholar's star, and he will bring fame to his family name. My wife has had half a lifetime of suffering, but things will change for the better in her old age. . . ."

Tears ran down my mother's face. Each word of the chants and lamentations was inscribed on my mother's heart, but she barely listened to his prophecies for her future.

"You were doing so well," my mother cut in. "How could you go just like that? Why do you keep coming into my dreams? What do you need help with? Tell me what it is and how I can help you."

The interruption seemed to rattle the shaman. He stopped chanting, stood silently for a long time, and then his whole body began to tremble. The shaman's assistant reprimanded her: "His connection to the spirit is very weak. If that connection is broken suddenly, the shaman might be harmed."

The shaman seemed to regain his composure and started chanting again, still channeling my father: "I should have lived many years longer, but bad luck caught up with me. The day I left your world, I had just stepped outside when five ghosts approached. One was red, and one was yellow, another blue, then a green one, and a purple one. . . . They saw that my hold on life was weak. They saw my disability and started to mock me. I lost my temper. I wasn't ready to leave, but they dragged me out of my body, punishing me for getting angry at them. . . ."

My mother began to wail and sob again. She was about to interrupt again, but the shaman's assistant stopped her.

"This was not meant to be my fate," the shaman continued. "I drifted for a while after I left my body. The gods knew I was from a faithful home, so they brought me to them and told me I must deal with what was left unfinished, that I must atone for my sins, but for now I walk aimlessly, not sure where I'm going. . . ."

"I'm going to do whatever it takes," my mother said, unable to hold back.

"Help me find my destination, help me find a way to atone."

"Tell me how."

My mother wanted to keep asking questions, but the shaman began to shudder again, and the assistant said, "He's already gone."

After all was said and done, we were led over to make the final donation of two hundred yuan. On the way home, my mother continued to weep, but for me the spell had been broken, and I wanted to explain the trick to her.

"I could tell right away it was fake," I started.

"I know it was your father. Stop."

"He must have gone out and got information about people who died in the area. . . ."

My mother waved me off. She didn't want to hear any of what I had to say. "I know he must have had some accident," she said. "We have to help him."

"I want to help him, too, but I don't believe in any of this. . . ."

"I believe it." My mother's expression made it clear that she wanted to end the conversation.

I knew that my mother needed to believe she was helping my father.

It helped to have friends in high places, and she stopped off at each temple to ask for divine help. She wanted to know how she could bring my father back to this world, if only temporarily. "We can only ask the gods for help," she explained, "but each god is in charge of a different thing, like in our world the Public Security Bureau is in charge of household registration. . . . So to track down a spirit, you need to go to the right god, which is the local god of wherever the spirit is from."

When I saw my mother rushing around looking for a solution to my father's spiritual problems, however strange it was to me, I could still understand what she was doing. But deep down, I couldn't shake the conclusion that she simply couldn't face her own grief. I could see her weakness.

She put everything into her quest, and I was at a loss as to what I should be doing. When I got back to my parents' house, I couldn't shake the feeling that something was missing. The feeling was still weak, like some faint smell in the air, but as time went by it seemed to gather around me and grow stronger. It felt as if it was festering inside me, almost like indigestion. I thought it must be what other people called grief.

My mother followed the local god's instructions and eventually came to tell me that on a particular date, we would be able to go to the temple of the local god and meet my father. "The local god found him," she said, "and he's on his way here now."

I had gone along with her plan until then, but I was suddenly tired of the charade. "You just want to find a way to make yourself feel better," I said.

She pretended not to hear me and continued: "So when

we get there, you have to stand in the doorway of the temple and call him, and then tell him to come home with you."

"You just want to find a way to comfort yourself."

"I need you to help me with this. The local god told me that I can't call him myself. You're his son—you have his blood in you."

The next day when we were supposed to leave, I couldn't contain my annoyance. When my mother saw, she chased after me and yelled, "You have to call him back!"

I didn't answer.

I didn't expect her to run after me. Her eyes were dry, but there were red circles around them. She wasn't sad; she was furious.

I had never lost the feeling of closeness with temples and gods, so when I got to the doorway of the local god's temple, even though it was the dwelling of a supernatural power, it felt more like dropping in on a family patriarch. Hokkien people have a local god for every district and village, and according to tradition, this god guides everyone in the community through life, intervening on their behalf with gods and demons, negotiating for heavenly blessings, and trying to head off potential disasters. The local god was responsible for all those things and more. Every year, locals led processions to the local god's temple, beating drums and gongs, carrying his statue in a sedan chair down roads and alleys spread with joss paper and medicinal herbs, taking him on a raucous inspection of every inch of his domain.

As my mother requested, I started by offering some incense at the altar to tell the city god I had arrived. I went back to the doorway and stood beside her.

She motioned for me to begin.

I opened my mouth but nothing came out.

My mother gave me an anxious nudge.

I opened my mouth again and finally yelled, "Dad! I'm here to get you, come home with me."

My shouts were swallowed up by silence. I hadn't expected a response.

My mother told me to keep yelling, while she went into the temple to use her moon blocks to ask the local god if my father had arrived.

I kept going, half-heartedly, listening to the sound of the clattering blocks from inside the temple.

I yelled until I couldn't take it anymore. I yelled until I choked on my words. I mumbled finally, "If you can really hear me, please come home. I miss you."

"Your father's here!" my mother shouted.

I started to cry.


In the days after my father was "drawn back," as my mother called it, there was a joyful atmosphere at home.

My mother cooked something new every day and put it all on the altar. She went to find an artisan who made paper funeral offerings and had him make her a paper cell phone and a cardboard motorcycle. Those were the two things my father had asked for after his stroke.

A few days later, she went back to her divine friends to ask them how she could go about helping my father atone for his sins. Their suggestion was for my father to act as a sort of volunteer for a local deity, like the American idea of sending minor offenders to do community service. "These gods are pretty modern, aren't they?" I joked.

My mother nodded and very solemnly said, "They have to keep up with the times, too."

A few days later, my mother found the perfect place for my father to do his divine community service: Zhenhai Temple at White Sands Village.

White Sands Village was a small community on the outskirts of my hometown that had become a tourist destination. The river that ran through the area made a dramatic turn right around the village, just before emptying into the ocean. The curve of the river had created a triangular patch of land rimmed with white sand. Whenever we went on field trips for school, we always went to White Sands Village.

Zhenhai Temple sat at the corner of the triangle, near the mouth of the river. I had noticed on a trip to White Sands when I was younger that local fishermen would cruise past, bowing to the temple before roaring out into the open ocean.

When my father worked on the ships, he used to make the trip out to Zhenhai Temple a few times a week to pray for safety on his voyages out to sea. "He came here thousands of times," my mother told me on our first visit there together, "so the gods here know him well. They'll take him in."

Arranging his passage to the temple was a simple procedure. My mother burned incense in front of our home altar and told the gods in the niche, "Zhenhai Temple has agreed to accept my husband as a helper. I want you to help me send him there." Then we picked up the offerings and rushed over to Zhenhai Temple.

I brought my mother there on my motorcycle. From our town to White Sands Village it was about fifteen miles. The ride took us along the beach, and when the wind picked up, we were blasted with sand. I was driving carefully and taking my time, which gave her time to reminisce. She pointed to a beach and said, "Your father and I came here to watch the sea." When we rode past a small restaurant, she said, "When your father was planning to go to Ningbo, he took me here for lunch."

When I walked into Zhenhai Temple, I was hit with the familiar scent of the place, an aroma I knew from childhood. Everything looked the same. A temple is a special type of place, I thought to myself, because whenever you return, it's always the same. The feeling of a temple never changes. I'm not sure what creates that solemn, warm atmosphere. Maybe it's from all those prayers mumbled in front of the altar, voices mixing and floating upward.

The head of the temple seemed to have been made aware of my father's situation. As soon as he saw my mother, he said warmly, "Your husband has arrived. I just got word from the gods." He put on some tea and passed cups to my mother and me. "Don't worry," he said. "They will look after him. They have known him since he was a boy."

The tea was very good, and the sun spilled bright white across the stone floor of the temple like whitecaps.

"What does he have to do?" my mother asked.

"Well," the head of the temple said, "he just got here. But they know he's a go-getter, so I suppose they'll probably have him running errands, taking messages around for them."

"But he can't really get around very well. He was half paralyzed before passing away, so he might hold things up."

"That doesn't matter. They have already fixed his leg. He may have gotten mixed up in some things that have not yet been resolved, but he was a good man, so the gods of the temple are happy to help him."

"That's good then," my mother said, her eyes half closed in a smile.

After that, the head of the temple and my mother swapped stories about my father's visits to the temple.

We sat for an entire afternoon. She knew she had to get home to make dinner, but she hesitated. Before she could allow herself to leave, she had to ask, "I don't want to make any trouble, but I just want to know how he's doing. Is he getting along okay? Is he busy?"

The head of the temple laughed and went to the altar.

"He was a bit clumsy at first," the head of the temple said, "and he had a few problems, but the gods are understanding."

My mother immediately rushed to the altar, bowing, and said, "Ask them to go easy on him! Please! My husband has always been clumsy." She lowered her voice and hissed at my father, "Come on, you! Be more careful. Don't cause any trouble."

Even after my father had begun his divine community service, my mother was still unable to find relief. The day after our first visit, she wanted me to take her back to the temple. It wasn't as if she could see him working, but she wanted to know how he was doing.

When we arrived, the head of the temple put on tea. The sun was as beautiful as it had been the day before. They chatted again about my father and the temple. And before she left, my mother once again couldn't help but ask about my father, so the head of the temple went to the altar to ask after him. The answer came: "He's making progress."

"Really?" my mother said. "Great. I'm proud of you. I'm going to make your favorite marinated duck for you and bring it over tomorrow." And then we drove the forty minutes back home again.

After lunch the following day, my mother wanted to go back again to deliver the duck. Her trips to Zhenhai Temple continued, and as the days went by, my father's performance was upgraded from "not bad" to "making progress," then to "the gods are very satisfied with him." Every time she went to Zhenhai Temple, she came back all smiles.

My mother had discussed with the gods the length of his community service, and the answer she received through her moon blocks was that he should spend at least a month at Zhenhai Temple, and then, if necessary, if his sins were not yet cleansed, transfer to another temple. But that would require another god and another temple to accept him.

That day, as we were preparing to go out after lunch, I saw my mother pacing nervously. The whole way there, she kept asking me, "Do you think he did a good job for them? I'm sure he made his share of mistakes, but they'll understand, right? Do you think he enjoyed himself?"

She didn't give me time to answer one question before she had asked the next.

We went into the temple and accepted cups of tea.

My mother wasn't in the mood to chat over her tea, though. "Did he complete his task?" she asked.

The head of the temple said, "Don't ask me. Rest here a while, wait until the sun goes down, then you can ask the gods yourself."

My mother couldn't spend another afternoon talking over tea. She moved her chair into the temple and sat, waiting for dusk, waiting for the sun to slip off the floor of the temple like the tide going out, and for my father to receive his judgment.

Maybe all the anxiety had exhausted her, because after a while, she fell asleep in the chair.

The sun sank behind the temple. It looked like a ripe orange tangerine as it slowly slipped into the ocean.

I gently shook my mother awake and said, "It's time to ask them."

She woke with a start, and I saw that she was smiling.

"I don't need to," she said.

My father had come to her, she said. She told me that he looked like he had when he was in his twenties. His skin was fair and smooth. His body looked strong, not yet beaten down by age and illness. He had his hair cut short. He moved gracefully. He waved to her, she said, and then he seemed to drift away from her, away from this world. She saw him fade into a silhouette and then into nothing.

"He's gone," my mother said. "He's finally at ease. He's gone."

Tears ran down my mother's face.

I knew that she was finally laying down her burden. It was not only tears leaving her body.

When we were about to leave, my mother turned back toward the temple and smiled at the gods inside.

I pressed my palms together reverently and mumbled, "Thank you. It's good to know she has friends in high places."

From that point on, I never stopped believing.

# 6

# Bella Zhang

Bella Zhang was beautiful. That was her name after all, but I only confirmed the fact much later.

Before I ever laid eyes on her, I knew the legend of Bella Zhang.

The trip to my elementary school and back was down a stone path that ran beside a slightly decrepit brick house. In the evening, when the flagstone path was illuminated with a sunset color of rouge, the pathway was particularly beautiful.

But that was also the hour when we often heard the sound of a woman sobbing coming from a brick house. It was less a sob than a plaintive wail rising and falling in the dusk. That is how the legend got started that the house was haunted. The ghost's name was Bella Zhang.

When I was young, I didn't really have it in me to figure out what it was. I suppose that is why I needed all those legendary tales of chivalrous fighters, seductive ghosts, and love.

At my school, the legend of Zhang spread like wildfire: it had all three of those elements.

Once upon a time, at least the way I heard it, Bella Zhang had been a sweet, beautiful girl. She fell in love with a man who worked on a freighter. He had come to town to load up on supplies. He was tall and well built, befitting his role as the legend's knight in shining armor. The idea of a girl losing her virginity before marriage was unimaginable in our small town, but Zhang made a secret rendezvous with the sailor and gave herself to him. They made a plan to elope, but their secret was discovered, and she was dragged home—and then killed herself.

The legend of Zhang was a cautionary tale. That was a time of great changes in coastal towns like ours. The streets began to glow with neon, and outsiders rushed in like the tide, patronizing the newly opened bars and peddling goods of dubious origin.

These great changes in our sleepy coastal town were an assault on the psychology of the locals. On one hand, they enjoyed hearing gossip from those brave enough to stride into the ballroom, savoring every detail, mouths agape at the descriptions of gold wallpaper, scandalized by the mention of short skirts exposing creamy thighs, but on the other hand, they were quick to offer their sanctimonious assessments of the excess and debauchery.

But what nobody realized was that with the coming of wealth and the steady churn of cash in town, it became impossible for people to contain their private desires. Without hunger and poverty to worry about, everyone could relax a bit. Poverty had acted like a valve, keeping private desires from gushing out, but with a bit of money, those wants and aspirations could flow freely. For the first time, everyone was forced to confront those desires.

It was an age of restlessness, stirring things up in the hearts of people—young and old, men and women. . . . The old folks would gather together and sigh deeply, saying, "We might have been poor before, but at least there wasn't as much to worry about." They nodded in agreement, but there was a fresh caution in the way they studied each other's faces.

Fortunately, we had the legend of Zhang. She represented what would happen to those who fell into disrepute. We stood safely back from the pit of desire, but she had already fallen in. The lesson was drilled into our heads, repeated over and over again. The details of her story could be put to use in explaining any number of unwritten rules: don't talk to outsiders, never meet secretly with a classmate of the opposite sex. . . . The list of forbidden behavior seemed to go on forever, extending even to a complete ban on going into the type of hair salons where a woman could get highlights in her hair. The point was always driven home like this: "Do you want to end up like Bella Zhang, with your reputation following you around town forever?"

Nobody expected that their attempts to demonize Zhang would make her into a saint.

Her legend only grew. There were harrowing tales of her preternatural powers of seduction, recollections of how she was caught in flagrante delicto with the man from the freighter, stories about how he was in fact the descendant of a grand general of the People's Liberation Army, and so on. . . . I had an image of her in my mind, but the details had not yet been filled in. Finally, the description that stuck was one offered by a classmate: "You know the girl leaning on the motorcycle in that nudie calendar? That's what Bella Zhang looks like."

Around that time, my male classmates and I began to have inexplicable urges. It was only later that words like "horny" or "sexual appetite" were applied to them. We started an underground circulation of dirty pictures. Thoughts of Zhang—legendary fallen woman but calendar girl doppelganger—especially when they came late at night, suddenly became less philosophical and more biological.

If our town could be said to have a goddess of sex—our own personal Venus—then it would have to be her. For a boy like me, obsessed with *Dream of the Red Chamber*, she was as seductive and ephemeral as the fairies that Jia Baoyu saw in his dream.

It was an age of turbulence. If parents saw a woman coming up the road who looked like she came from outside of our town—wearing fancy clothes, hair dyed—they would leap to cover their children's eyes as if sheltering them from some horrific sight. But within a couple of years, local women started to adopt the same fashions. Otherwise how could they compete with those women coming from outside our town who were looking to steal their husbands away from them?

The sight of men shouting into cell phones became commonplace. More women came, too, parading around in the latest fashions, faces caked with heavy makeup.

The legend of Zhang fell by the wayside. She was outshone by the neon glow, and her legend was replaced by stories of the "princesses" that filled the streets of our town. No longer was sobbing heard from the old brick house.

I was no exception. She had once been so vivid in my imagination that I felt as if I knew her face. But it seemed on the verge of disappearing completely.

My curiosity did not fade, though. I decided to recruit Piggie from down the street to go on a stakeout with me. We got together flashlights, slingshots, a stack of Daoist paper charms, and a peachwood sword that Piggie borrowed from his grandfather (he was a Daoist priest who specialized in dealing with departed souls who needed a push into the afterlife). When we were halfway to the old brick house, Piggie asked me why we were going to investigate. I didn't have an answer for him. After a long pause, I finally said, "You want to see her, too, don't you?"

"Of course I do," Piggie said hesitantly, "but I'm scared."

We started walking up the path.

As we got closer to the house, an inexplicable sensation rushed through me, rocketing through my body and settling somewhere around my crotch. I had finally figured out why exactly I wanted to investigate the house, and I could barely contain my excitement.

Piggie gave the door to the house a gentle nudge with the peachwood sword, and we immediately heard the sound of two women talking inside. I peered in through the crack in the door and saw a pale, thin face. It seemed to be staring directly at me. "It's a ghost," Piggie yelled as he ran down the path.

At that moment, I was sure it was a ghost, too. I ran home and locked the door behind me as soon as I got inside. My heart was thudding in my chest. I looked down and noticed another biological response poking up through my pants. I didn't dare tell anyone at home what had happened on the stakeout. The pale face I had seen through the crack in the door would not go away. As time went by, it seemed to become more concrete. The face resolved itself, and a pair of eyes blinked back at me. It seemed like the expression the face wore was meant to put me at ease, as if it was encouraging me to gaze at it in my mind's eye.

For the next few days, I wasn't myself. When I spaced out and dropped my chopsticks for the third time at dinner, my mother gave me a rap on the skull and said, "Did you see a ghost or something?"

It was a casual remark—but that was exactly what I was worried about. Was it a ghost I had seen in that house?

I panicked whenever the face floated into my consciousness. Without telling my parents, I went to the temple to get another stack of paper charms, which I stuck all over myself. The face kept returning, though.

One day, the face turned toward me and smiled.

It was torture. I could barely sleep, and when I did, I would shudder awake from wet dreams. My body couldn't hold out much longer. One afternoon, I finally worked up the courage to tell my mother what was happening, to admit to her that I was being haunted by a female ghost.

Before I got the chance to tell her, though, my mother came bounding into the room with a wedding invitation. "That Bella Zhang down the street is finally getting married," she said happily.

"Isn't she dead?" I asked.

"What are you talking about? I can't forgive what she did, of course. I think everyone around here thought she'd be better off if she *did* die. But it seems like things worked out okay for her. That guy ended up going into business for himself, made out pretty good, and now he's back to get her. Her parents might never recover from what she put them through. Just imagine having a daughter like that— but I guess things turned out okay."

The wedding was extravagant for the time, but it was also unusually sloppy.

The wedding gifts were arranged according to local

custom, and everything was more than covered. Bags of fancy candy were sent around the neighborhood, and the wedding banquet was in the finest hotel in town. But Zhang and the mysterious groom only appeared briefly, offering a perfunctory toast to the assembled guests before quickly retreating to the private room reserved for close family.

The next day, she left for her husband's hometown in the northeast.

I didn't know much about the northeast except that it was directly north of our town. I used to stand out on the main road looking north and imagine walking until I saw her.

I always thought I would meet her again. I didn't want to fail to recognize her when that moment came, so I did my best to recall her face.

Memory is like water, though. The more I dipped in to retrieve her face, the cloudier the water became, until one day I realized it had disappeared completely.

There's no sense trying to fight it, I told myself disconsolately. I decided to try memorializing those years in poetry.

The sad fact is that bookworms like me never truly experience or understand the full glory of youth.

Bella Zhang, on the other hand—she had *lived*.

Two years after the wedding, she arrived back in our town, wearing a *qipao* split up the thighs, her hair done in the latest fashion, her neck wrapped in gold necklaces, and her fingers full of rings.

I heard that she arrived in a luxury car, but I wasn't there to experience her grand return, since I was stuck in class. I kept imagining the scene, picturing adoring crowds lining her route.

A few days after her return, rumors started to spread that she had divorced. That was the only reason she had come back.

What did that really mean, though? Divorce was virtually unknown where I came from, and most people only had the vaguest idea what it signified.

Shortly after that, a shop opened across from my school. There were streamers out front and a rotating red light. The neighbors said that Zhang had opened it.

Rumor had it that she was only home three days before her family kicked her out of the house. That was when she moved in at her new location. The only thing I was sure of was that the red light out front of the shop was on for three days before an announcement appeared, pasted up in the alley, bearing a message written with ink and brush: "From this day forward, our family and Bella Zhang have severed all ties. We take no responsibility for her, no matter what happens."

The characters on the proclamation were beautiful, written with force and vigor. They were clearly written by a family elder with some talent for calligraphy. They were evidence of the refined, scholarly family that had produced Zhang. But their beauty was lost on the crowd that formed to gawk at the proclamation with barely concealed glee.

I had to go by the shop every day on my way to school, but when I passed around seven in the morning, the door was tightly shut. I noticed a few notes pasted up on the storefront and wanted to go over to look, but I could never work up the nerve. A week later, I got up at five thirty and rode my bike over. The notes, covered in messy scrawl, had been pasted up crookedly across the door of the shop. "Filthy bitch," one read, another, "Whore," and a third, "Kill yourself, slut."

I read the notes while constantly glancing over my shoulder to see if anyone was coming. When someone finally appeared in the alley, I fled, pedaling into the school yard.

What kind of shop did she open? The attempts to answer that question only added to her legend.

Debauchery on a grand scale, someone said. Don't judge the place by the storefront—open that door and you can go down two more floors, pretty girls just waiting to satisfy any desires.

Another theory was that it was a luxury massage parlor. There were imported massage tables, they said, and the therapists could work you over until you were too limp to get up.

Every night, the boys in the dormitory batted around theories and rumors, getting more and more worked up, until suddenly everyone found an excuse for privacy.

Around that time, Big Boy—that was our nickname for Zhang's ex-husband—showed up in town.

It was just a rumor at first, and most people found it in-credible, but Big Boy started to appear in front of the shop every evening, leaning back in a chair, enjoying the cool night air.

We started to hear fighting and dishes breaking in the middle of the night. But the next day at dusk, Big Boy would appear again, dragging his chair out in front of the shop as if nothing had happened.

Nobody knew what was happening inside; maybe even Zhang and Big Boy couldn't have explained it. But finally, one day the doors swung open. The streamers and the red light had been taken down. A sign replaced them: Bella's Seafood Restaurant.

The sign signaled the debut of a new Bella Zhang who went around with her head held high, smiling warmly as she greeted customers at the front counter of her restaurant. Locals vowed never to step foot in Bella's Seafood Restau-rant, but she had plenty of business from the out-of-town folks who worked on the freighters and came to do busi-ness in town.

Inspecting the shop from across the street, I could see it really was her restaurant: just like her, it seemed completely out of place in our little town. There was gold-trimmed furniture, glittering curtains of glass beads, and leather chairs, and all the waitresses were tall, pretty out-of-town girls. It was brimming with what our neighbors disapprov-ingly termed a "seductive atmosphere."

Zhang's restaurant and our town seemed to stand in

opposition to each other. She was symbolic of a corrosive element that was wearing away the character of the town.

If there was a war between her and the town, she won without ever firing a shot. Her restaurant was successful enough that it began to expand and take over neighboring storefronts, and gradually, local businessmen found themselves "unable to resist" Bella's Seafood Restaurant.

"What're you gonna do?" the businessmen would say, by way of explanation, after giving a vivid description of the dining room. "When my clients come to town, they want me to take them there."

Not long after that, there was another victory for her: a local big shot was planning his son's wedding and decided to book the dining room of Bella's Seafood Restaurant.

My father had gotten an invitation to the wedding, and when the big day came, I paced nervously around the house. When he received the invitation, the point was made to him that this restaurant was the best place in town to make connections with non-local businessmen.

I volunteered to go with him, but my mother intervened with a fierce refusal. I watched from the window, tracing my father's path up to the restaurant. He hesitated for a moment before going inside.

"Amazing food." That was the only assessment my father offered upon returning from the wedding. That was all he—and everyone else in town—felt comfortable commenting on. It was the quality of the food that finally got everyone to put aside their jealousy and forget about town politics. Finally our town was seemingly embracing Bella Zhang.

When it came time to renovate some buildings at the school, local patriarchs went around for donations. They visited Old John, who had opened a shop in town, but he hesitated to contribute, and Old Tom, who owned an electrical appliance store, wouldn't commit either. Zhang was happy to pitch in. She marched right over to the school, invited herself into the principal's office, and said, "Put me down for fifty thousand."

At the time, fifty thousand yuan was a considerable sum. It was enough to build a house in town.

The principal was hesitant, though. "I'll have to think it over," he said.

When the list of donors was released, her name was nowhere to be found.

Not long after that, the local patriarchs were raising money to renovate an ancestral hall, and she stepped up again. However, when the list of donors was published, her name had been left off again.

As the New Year approached, the Mazu temple announced a project to expand its courtyard. Finally she found someone to take her money.

Carved on a wall inside the temple was the entry "From devout woman Bella Zhang: fifty thousand yuan." It was the largest donation the temple had received, but her name appeared at the bottom of the list. She wasn't discouraged by the placement, though. After that, she went often to the temple to stroll in the newly expanded square and then bend down to admire the carved entry.

I often hung around the grocery store next to the Mazu temple, watching her smile open like a flower blossoming.

By the time I went off to high school, she had become the vice president of the town's Entrepreneurs Association. Her seafood restaurant had relocated to a five-story building near the estuary.

That year, the banquet for outstanding students at our high school was sponsored by her and held at her restaurant. She made a speech afterward, hitting all the talking points about giving service to the motherland and building the nation.

By that time, she was no longer a young woman. She had a double chin, and a thick layer of foundation could not cover the wrinkles that had begun to creep upward across her face. She was still beautiful, though.

The local patriarchs were not pleased with the school's decision to accept her support. At that point, she had diversified her business and opened up Seaside Entertainment City next to the restaurant.

Word of the leisure complex had spread up and down the coast. I wasn't sure exactly what went on there, but I heard there was a concert hall, a ballroom, a café, and private rooms for karaoke. There were also rumors of some "less than legitimate" businesses operating out of Seaside Entertainment

City—the most popular of those rumors, at least at my high school, was that drugs were being sold there. When a classmate abruptly left school that year, some speculated that he had gotten an STD from a visit to the entertainment complex.

We received repeated admonitions from principals and senior teachers to stay away; parents informed their children in hushed tones about the disgusting goings-on at the complex; and I realized that the town's latest crusade against Zhang was just beginning.

On the day of the student banquet, my gaze followed the wall that separated the restaurant from Seaside Entertainment City. I couldn't stop myself from wandering over to the window again and again, hoping to catch a glimpse of what was happening on the other side.

It was a massive complex. I guessed the big building in the center must be the ballroom. It was surrounded by European-style villas. I had heard that each villa had a different theme: in one was a bar to hear slow jams and ballads, another was a disco, and another was a fancy café.

After the dinner, I was chosen as the student journalist who would interview Outstanding Entrepreneur Bella Zhang.

I was going to interview her in her office.

She was wearing black stockings and a business dress. I couldn't manage to get a word out. I was sweating bullets. It was my first time talking to her.

The teacher that accompanied me reminded me that I didn't need to take notes. It was simply a formality.

I knew she was used to this kind of ceremonial gesture. But it was in such ceremonies that she was finally being recognized for what she had done. I mumbled my way through my dull questions, asking her things like "What advice would you like to give to students?" She did her best to say all the things she imagined a woman in her position would say.

She seemed satisfied with how the interview was going. Halfway through, out of nowhere, she pledged some funds to support school journalists. She and the teacher shook hands. It was a success.

As I was leaving the office, I shut the door behind me, but I couldn't resist one last look. I caught her as she deflated, her head leaned back, slouched in her massive office chair. Her expression betrayed an indescribable fatigue.

The more we were pressured to stay away from Seaside Entertainment City, the more we wanted to get inside. One of my classmates couldn't wait any longer. He secretly slipped inside and came back to tell us about all the "awesome" things he had seen.

In my group at school, if you had the guts to sneak inside, it was a mark of pride. And outside school, if your parents found out about a trip to the complex, it was a mark of shame.

More rumors began to spread: we heard that the complex was overseen by four gangsters, each with his own horrible specialty, and they were planning to begin recruiting at our school.

I never really believed that story. Even if there were gangs operating there, getting involved with the school would only bring unwanted scrutiny. I suspected that some people who worked at the complex had big mouths, and maybe they had organized their own little groups, too. But whatever rumors were spreading in town, they all seemed to be about Seaside Entertainment City.

There was growing anger. It started with the town patriarchs and spread to the women's auxiliaries, and they started to visit every household in town and press them to sign petitions against the complex. Zhang did not admit defeat, though, and launched her own counterstrike. When the town government announced that they were starting renovations on their offices, she showed up with a donation of two hundred thousand yuan.

It was right back to the cold war between the town's residents and Zhang. The situation was a tinderbox, and everyone was waiting for a stray spark to set the whole thing alight.

The spark came during summer vacation in my third year of high school. A fight broke out at Seaside Entertainment City. A man was beaten to death. He was the son of a powerful local patriarch.

A gang of locals showed up at the front gate and started shouting abuse and hurling stones. They demanded that Seaside Entertainment City be immediately shut down.

I took advantage of my student reporter credentials and rushed to the scene.

The crowd had grown to include young and old, people directly involved in the fight and the protest as well as curious onlookers. They were shouting the same words I had read on those notes: "Filthy bitch," "Whore," "Kill yourself, slut." Zhang appeared on the roof of the main building. She raised a megaphone and yelled down to the crowd: "It was an accident. This is my town, too. Please, you have to know that I want to make it right."

She didn't make it through the speech before people began pelting her with stones.

She was too high up to be in any danger, and the rocks thudded against the building.

The crowd parted to allow her mother to pass. She walked unsteadily forward and wailed up at her daughter, "You didn't bring anything but bad luck! Why couldn't you have just died instead? Why did you have to come back just to curse us?"

It seemed that it had been a long time since Zhang and her mother had seen each other. Zhang raised the megaphone and yelled down, "You have to believe me, Mama. I swear I never did anything I should be ashamed of. I really haven't."

Her mother looked on the verge of collapse. "You were a curse," she said. "That's all you were. I should have strangled you to death when I had the chance."

Big Boy arrived on the roof and pulled Zhang back inside.

The shouts and curses kept up for a while and then slowly faded.

Things were quiet overnight, but when I got up the next morning, I learned that Zhang had gone to her family's ancestral shrine. She knelt down and swore to heaven that she had never committed any unforgivable sins. "I was looking for someone to love me," she sobbed. "I never sold my body and I never sold drugs. I did what I thought would make me happy, what I thought was right, and I built a business. But I never did anything unforgivable."

When she had finished crying, she smashed her head into the stone wall of the hall.

The next day, the family patriarchs woke up to find her there. She was dead. The blood, already congealed in the dust, looked like ancient incense ash.

According to local custom, funeral ceremonies should take place at the home of the deceased or in the ancestral hall. After burial, a wooden plaque carved with the name of the deceased went up in the hall, marking their passage. It was said that without the plaque the soul of the deceased could not rest.

But neither Zhang's family nor the Zhang ancestral hall was willing to take the body. There was no chance a plaque would be put up for her either. Her spirit would wander forever. That was the most extreme punishment anyone could have wished on her.

She would wander once again with nobody to claim her as their own.

In the end, Big Boy took care of the arrangements. He planned a solemn send-off for her, which her family and everyone else in town shunned. He sent for a band from a neighboring town, and they played the wailing funeral tunes for three days and three nights.

When the music had finished, Big Boy sent everyone away, and then he set fire to Seaside Entertainment City.

Nobody called for help. No fire engines came to put out the blaze. Everyone watched impassively as the place burned. When the fire had burned to coals, some people came out to set off firecrackers. That was the tradition in our town: if a family member who had been sick regained their health, the news was greeted with fireworks.

Six years after I graduated from university, one of my high school classmates who had done well for himself in business organized a ten-year reunion. He sent my invitation to Beijing. I opened the red envelope to find that the location was Seaside Entertainment City.

I hadn't spent much time back home since going off to university, so I was completely unaware that the place had reopened.

This later iteration of Seaside Entertainment City was completely different. The villas had been rebuilt, but the central building had been replaced with a wide green lawn. The atmosphere was festive, with speakers pumping in music, everyone dressed up and greeting each other warmly.

I arrived late, and everyone had already assembled. I told myself not to, but I couldn't help asking: "Why did they rebuild this place?"

The classmate who had organized the reunion laughed hollowly. "Where there is demand," he said, "there will always be supply. The town has money now, and people need somewhere to spend it."

I wanted to drop it, but he kept going.

"Business is fueled by desire," he said. "Currency is king."

Once we were a few rounds deep, a couple of classmates started to tease me for my childhood obsession with Zhang. "She was the girl of your dreams, wasn't she?"

I blushed. I didn't know what to say. Someone else hooted, "What are you blushing for? You weren't the only one!"

Someone proposed a toast to her, and the classmate who had just given me the impromptu lesson on the business of desire cut in. "This was a hot-blooded generation, and we all owe a debt to the one who got our blood pumping in the first place, the founder of a new movement of aesthetic appreciation, a sexual revolution. . . ."

Everyone joined in enthusiastically: "To the great Bella Zhang!"

I couldn't bring myself to join in. I went to stand alone

for a while, looking out at the lawn. I thought about the old brick house and the pale face that had haunted my thoughts for days. "I guess she never could escape trying to be a good girl," I said to myself. "That's why she killed herself."

Behind me the party continued, and people began swapping stories about Seaside Entertainment City and its founder.

I couldn't take it. I smashed my glass on the ground and stormed out. I kept going until I couldn't see that disgusting place anymore.

# 7

# Tiny and Tiny

There were two Tinys, but until fifth grade, I only knew one of them. His house was across from mine.

It was a standard Hokkien house: two central buildings arranged on either side of a worship hall. The hall was for praying to gods and making offerings to the spirits of ancestors, and it was quite normal in our part of southern Fujian, where there are so many gods and so many festivals that it felt like keeping up with spiritual affairs was a full-time job.

In most traditional houses in southern Fujian, there were two separate wings as well, with a courtyard in the middle. But Tiny's family had not had the resources to complete the project, so instead of that, there was a small yard surrounded by palm trees, and then a larger backyard, overgrown with tall grass, where the family kept a large black dog.

Tiny's was a typical fisherman's family. His father had been making a living from the sea since he was a boy, and

Tiny's two older brothers both went to work with him as soon as they finished elementary school. His mother was in charge of mending nets and taking the catch to the market to sell. It looked like Tiny would follow the same path as his brothers, but before finishing elementary school, he often vowed, "I'm never going to be a fisherman."

Tiny's mother was named Wuxi. I was quite fond of her. Every time my mother and I went over for a visit, we were guaranteed a seafood dinner. Wuxi laughed as if she had known no emotion in her life but unbridled joy. Whenever she saw me, she would find some treat to press on me, and when she stopped by to see us, she always brought some fish or shrimp. Tiny's father and older brothers always called out to me when I passed and joked around with me, and even the family's dog wagged his tail when he saw me coming down the alley.

But Tiny always seemed to keep to himself, usually hiding away in a quiet corner of the house when we stopped by. Our two families might have been close, but Tiny wanted nothing to do with us. He was a quiet boy, and it seemed that there was something profound in his silence, as if he were absorbed in thought, a million miles away from what was going on around him. The only time he ever really talked to me was when he overheard my mother telling Wuxi that I had finished at the top of the class. He called me over and said, "Keep it up, Blackie. Study hard and get out of this little town."

I never thought of my hometown as little, and I had

never felt the urge to escape. But I admired him: someone who looked down on our little town must have his eyes set on the horizon. But he wasn't a very good student, so I decided his arrogant silence was probably just some kind of loneliness.

Tiny the Weirdo—that's what our neighbors called him.

That was when the next Tiny was chauffeured into my life in the backseat of a luxury sedan.

He arrived one afternoon at the entrance to the alley, in a type of car I had only ever seen on TV. There was no way that car could fit down the narrow lane, and as the driver tried to back out again, he ended up spraying the onlookers with clouds of dust.

I was watching, too, standing barefoot in the crowd. Back then, white sneakers and sailor suit school uniforms were popular, but I hated encasing my feet in a pair of sticky, sweaty sneakers. But our teacher had warned us that we only had two choices: sneakers or nothing, so I chose to go barefoot. I would toss my sneakers in my bag and walk around shoeless. It didn't matter if it was a hot summer day or pouring down rain. I grew thick calluses on my soles, so I could walk across broken glass without getting cut. My classmates nicknamed me the Barefoot Immortal, after a Daoist god who went everywhere without shoes.

There were no white sneakers for the Tiny who stepped out of the back of that luxury sedan, and you would never catch him going barefoot. He had on sharp dress shoes, like you would imagine a kid on TV wearing—and it wasn't just the shoes! He had suspenders and pressed pants, a tidy hair-cut to match, and a shirt that gleamed as white as his cheeks.

He looked like the stereotypical son of a rich family. He shone so bright that the rest of us looked gray in comparison.

He was the nephew of Auntie Yue, who lived to the east of us. Auntie Yue's older brother and his wife had headed to Hong Kong to work on a construction project. They had already completed the immigration procedures for themselves and their eldest son, but it would take a cou-ple of years before they could finally send for Tiny.

The neighborhood decided that the perfect nickname for this Tiny was Hong Kong Tiny, which made it sound like Hong Kong was his last name, or Tiny the Hong Konger.

Tiny the Hong Konger gave us wild neighborhood kids a feeling like what I imagine the Native Americans felt when the Europeans arrived on their shores.

The boy and his foster family were surrounded by a group of voyeuristic children as soon as he arrived. They were curious about everything that Tiny did. They noticed that when he spoke, he liked to raise his eyebrows to punc-tuate points. They marveled at his haircut, modeled on the floppy style of Hong Kong singer Aaron Kwok. He liked to whistle, too, and he took several baths a day. It wasn't long before the wild kids of the neighborhood were going around whistling and parting their hair off-center like Aaron Kwok. Some of the kids even peeked at him taking a bath, so they could study for themselves how sophisticated boys bathed.

Tiny's family was a little better off than most in the

neighborhood. At the time, it was the only family with a two-story house. Whenever his aunt washed his T-shirts and underwear, she hung them up to dry on the roof. Their dazzling white was like a banner of civilization waving arrogantly over our small town. For us kids, these clothes had another meaning, too, signaling something that stirred us hormonally. Within a matter of days after Tiny had arrived, a boy in the neighborhood clambered up an electrical pole hoping to catch sight of secrets that he kept even closer to his skin. The boy ended up slipping off the pole, but fortunately, he fell on turf rather than the cruel concrete that covers everything now. He escaped with nothing more serious than a scar.

Nobody in our town wanted rumors like that to spread, and the adults made like nothing out of the ordinary was going on. If something did happen, they pretended not to see it, or they pretended not to understand it. They stuck by their own uncomplicated ways of life no matter what happened.

Even before I met him, I came to the conclusion that I probably wouldn't like Tiny the Hong Konger. In the battalion of neighborhood kids who raced around the neighborhood in our flip-flops, I was known as the best student, and I was worried that Tiny might end up stealing away some of the attention I received from the neighbors. I wasn't ready to step out of the limelight.

I pretended not to pay any mind to Tiny and his devoted fans and voyeurs, but one day Auntie Yue came by and decided to throw us together. "You're a good student," she said, "so I want you to look after him. I don't want him being led astray by those wild boys."

Our first meeting was a bit awkward. My palms were sweaty, and I could barely get a word out without stuttering. Tiny, though, was the picture of cool.

He was wearing a shirt that seemed as white as snow, and he smelled like cologne. "My name is Tiny," he said, smiling to reveal gleaming white teeth. "I heard you finished top of your class."

I nodded.

"You're two years older than me, right?"

I nodded.

"It's a pleasure to meet you, Brother Blackie," he said, putting a formal address ahead of my nickname.

When I got back home, the Flip-Flop Army was waiting for me. They swarmed around me like flies buzzing in my ears. They wanted to know what Tiny was like, but I only answered, with fake solemnity, "He's a fine fellow and a complicated man." He had made a deep impression on me; he seemed to be a good person.

Tiny's family had contracted two bodyguards—both his cousins—for the boy, and they were charged with keeping him company and protecting him from negative influences. One of the cousins was tall and skinny, the other short and fat. Tiny only spoke to them to give orders, commands to get this or that for him. I'm not sure exactly what Tiny saw in me, but after our first meeting, his cousins often summoned me for an audience with him. They would arrive with invitations: "Do you want to come over and play marbles?" "Tiny wants to play hide-and-seek with you—you up for it?" "Tiny wants to know if you want to come over to play checkers."

The Flip-Flop Army was scared they would lose me. Whenever Tiny's cousins came with an invitation, they presented a counteroffer. I was caught in the middle and forced to choose a side.

At first, I wasn't ready to make a permanent choice. One day Tiny's cousin stopped by to say, "Tiny wants to know if you could come by to read some comic books he just got from Hong Kong, or play Nintendo. . . ."

That was how Tiny won me over. On that day, the Flip-Flop Army gave me a dishonorable discharge.

Tiny was a great playmate. He had all the latest things a kid could want—manga, computer games, puzzles, blocks—and he had two bodyguards to assist us. When we were thirsty, we could send them for cold drinks (brought from Hong Kong), and when we were hot, we could have them put on the electric fan (also brought from Hong Kong).

When it came to his cousins, Tiny was like a tyrannical landlord's son. He only needed to shoot them a glance to send them scurrying away. He didn't mind when I beat him at our games, but whenever his cousins didn't lose on purpose, he would scold them into submission.

The Flip-Flop Army watched from a short distance away. They would take paper tubes and yell at me, "Traitor, flunky . . ." I took it in stride and didn't bother answering them, but Tiny would march over to yell at them, "What are you wild boys yelling about?"

I realized that hostilities had commenced.

The Flip-Flop Army had a powerful weapon at its disposal. Their manure time bomb was advanced technology. The firecracker that provided the charge had a long fuse that took a minute to burn down. The trick was putting the firecracker in a lump of cow manure, then timing the explosion to go off just as Tiny and I arrived within range—and then cover us with manure.

I was familiar with their tricks, and it only took a few manure-time-bomb attacks before we learned to avoid them. However, the Flip-Flop Army was not prepared to admit defeat. Instead of planting firecrackers in manure for guerrilla attacks, they decided it would be easier to simply toss them at us. Tiny was furious. He ran inside and emerged with the shotgun the family kept to hunt birds. He pointed it at the sky and let off a shot.

*Bang!* The sound was like a wave crashing. It echoed in the ears of the Flip-Flop Army. They looked at Tiny in stunned silence. I was taken aback, too.

"I scared you, didn't I, you little beggars?" His gleaming white teeth flashed as he roared at them. It gave me chills.

Maybe I was scared to lose my ties to the Flip-Flop Army or maybe I wasn't comfortable with Tiny's arrogance, but after the shooting incident, I decided it was time to find some balance. Tiny and I had been joined at the hip, and I knew it was time to start splitting myself between the two cliques.

Tiny realized that my loyalties were divided, so he took out all his Hong Kong treasures to entice me back—his Hong Kong CDs, his Hong Kong remote-controlled plane. . . . But he knew that a gulf had opened up between us. "If you want to come over," he said finally, "go ahead, but it's fine if you don't want to."

I knew that he wanted to end our friendship before he was forced to admit that he had lost me.

I started to feel sorry for him. When I got to know him, I realized how lonely he was. It was his parents' fault. They were keeping him in perpetual limbo. He was always "preparing to go to Hong Kong." With everything in constant flux, there was no way for him to live in the moment or to have friendships.

Back then, Hong Kong seemed like a different, better world. That was Tiny's eventual destination, so maybe he thought he could look down on our small town.

He was still a kid, though, and a kid needs friends.

I decided he must have chosen me to be his friend because I was the best student. He couldn't look down on me in that regard. I was above him. And maybe winning me over would represent a conquest.

In the days after our friendship cooled, he often took out pictures of his older brother to show me.

Pictures were about the only way he could see his brother. Tiny was spoiled by his mother, and she couldn't stand the thought of him accompanying her to Hong Kong, where times for the family were tough. She sent Tiny to family in her hometown and mailed a thick stack of bills to them each month to look after him. But Tiny's older brother went along to Hong Kong to work on the jobsite.

Tiny's older brother grew up in Hong Kong; he became a Hong Konger, and he looked like a Hong Konger, with long hair and an earring, shorts and loafers, and sometimes even a silk scarf.

Of course, Tiny worshipped his brother, just like we all worshipped the fancy people we watched running between skyscrapers on our black-and-white TVs. Maybe both of us were simply worshipping our imaginary Hong Kongs.

For us, those skyscrapers belonged to a distant place, but for Tiny they were his future.

Tiny tried to grow his hair long, but his grandfather cut it off. He tried to use a needle to pierce his ear but ended up covered in blood, and his grandfather had to rush him to the hospital. He gave up on looking like a Hong Konger, but he kept quietly mooning over his brother's photos.


I tried to keep my distance from Tiny, but sometimes I would take a break from running the alley with the Flip-

Flop Army to pay him a visit. He always wanted to talk about his brother. "He's a hell of a guy," Tiny said. "They should put him on TV—he's the same as all those people. He's got a motorcycle and he drag-races on it with a girl on the back. But when it's time to go to work, he changes completely. You should see how sophisticated he looks with a suit on."

"My brother takes drugs," Tiny said to me one day, out of nowhere. He passed me a cigarette, then he leaned in and said, "That's exactly what this is." He looked pleased with himself, as if he had found the key to everything.

He took the cigarette back, wrapped it up in the handkerchief he had taken it from, then put the package in a metal box and slid it under his bed. I could tell he considered it his greatest treasure.

As I looked at him, I felt more distant from him than ever. I knew there was a passion inside him, and it frightened me. He wanted to leave this town and go to the city, to Hong Kong. He wanted to live how he imagined Hong Kongers lived.

I will admit, I had my own yearnings when I saw those skyscrapers on TV. But that city and those buildings were never truly real to me. They were too distant. Tiny was living between worlds. He was a man out of time, surrounding himself with the trappings of a city that seemed to be dozens of years ahead of our small town.

It wasn't completely unexpected when Tiny called me over one night and took me to his room to show me a bundle of money and ask where he could buy a motorcycle. "Like the ones on TV," he said. "I want you to take me to get one. I want to go drag racing."

Back then, there wasn't anywhere in our small town to buy a motorcycle. He would have had to make a trip forty miles into the city. "What about drugs?" he asked desperately. "Can we get some marijuana?"

That night I went along with him to an underground arcade where he played the slot machines. I watched him sit in front of a slot machine, stack up his tokens, then quickly lose them all. I vowed again to keep my distance from Tiny.

I could see that he was too invested in his fantasy. I was worried that I would be swallowed up by it, too.

I sensed a similar recklessness in myself.

It never occurred to me that Tiny and Tiny would become friends.

Tiny stopped sending over his cousins to get me, and I no longer stopped by to check on him. But one day his aunt sent for me. She wanted me to tutor him in math. He had scored 12 percent on his last exam.

I took the exam paper from her and went toward his room, planning to laugh in his face. He couldn't even do the basics, like adding a half to a third!

I went in and saw the fisherman's son and the future son of Hong Kong—Tiny and Tiny.

They were bent over a wooden dinosaur model.

It was a surprise. I had never seen the fisherman's son

speak more than three sentences to a stranger, but there he was, giving an exaggerated laugh, cooing over the dinosaur. "Wow! This is so cool. It looks like it could come to life."

I could tell he was sucking up. I felt an indescribable revulsion and a strange sadness watching my hometown Tiny become a sycophant. I knew what he saw in his namesake: Tiny could smell the sophisticated aroma of distant Hong Kong on his playmate.

I worked with Tiny on his math exam, showed him what he had done wrong, and got away as fast as I could.

Tiny chased after me, asking if I wanted to play a video game he had just gotten from Hong Kong. The fisherman's son was right behind him.

The way Tiny the fisherman's son smiled obsequiously over Tiny the Hong Konger's shoulder made me sick. "That's okay," I said. "I'm fine." I turned and left.

After that night, when Tiny's aunt asked me to tutor him, I would make up an excuse not to go.

I didn't want to see the fisherman's son. He was simple and small-minded, but he also made me realize how simple and small-minded I could be, too.

The Tiny I had known since I was young started to change. He skipped school for three weeks straight but headed off to school each morning and came back in the evening as usual. He went off to the town's new industrial zone to pick fights with the migrant workers, telling them to bark like a dog, then smacking them. Then one day his parents realized that he had sneaked into their room and stolen a few hundred yuan.

Wuxi was unhappy, but she didn't want to cry in front of her husband, so she went to see my mother.

"Boys will be boys," my mother said, trying to comfort her in the only way she knew how.

I listened, not speaking. I knew that Tiny and Tiny were both sick with the same illness: Hong Kong syndrome. I ran into the fisherman's son a few times in those days, and I noticed that even his voice had changed. He was wearing his hair in the same style as Tiny the Hong Konger. He was even copying his smile.

Finally I couldn't hold back. "Tell him to quit hanging out with that other Tiny," I told Wuxi.

She was stunned. She had been proud of her son for making friends with the sophisticated city-bound Tiny. My mother gave me a slap. "Quiet," she said, "adults are talking."

But Wuxi must have listened, because the next time I saw Tiny and Tiny, one of them gave me the cold shoulder and the other wanted a fight. It was the fisherman's son who motioned for me to square off.

The Flip-Flop Army stuck with me, though. There was relative peace. That was the end of things. I cut all ties with Tiny and Tiny.

I still heard rumors, though. My hometown Tiny ended up in a fight, got put in detention, then ended up being put on special monitoring. Finally he dropped out completely.

And then I heard that Tiny was finally headed to Hong Kong. It was only a week before he would leave our town forever.

Auntie Yue came by with the dinosaur model and a Nintendo console. Those were Tiny's favorite toys, and he wanted me to have them.

"I don't know what happened between you two," she said, "but he still likes you. You should stop by and see him if you can."

Tiny seemed to have been practicing for my visit. The self-satisfied expression he gave me when I walked in must have been the result of countless rehearsals.

He put a hand on my shoulder and pulled me closer. I felt like we were in a movie. He sat down on the bed and took out a scrap of paper. There was an address clumsily scrawled on it.

"You're the only person I'm giving this to," Tiny said. "I want you to write me if you can." He raised his eyebrows.

"A letter to Hong Kong, huh?" I said awkwardly, not sure exactly how to respond. "That's airmail, right? It'll be pretty expensive."

"We're friends," he said. "If it matters that much to you, you can come visit me in Hong Kong and I'll pay you back."

I passed him the gift I had brought him. It was a thick

physics textbook that I loved. I had saved up for six months to buy it.

"Auntie Yue showed me your physics homework," I said. "It was a mess. Do the practice exercises in here."

"What a crappy gift," he said, his arrogance as potent as ever.

He left for Hong Kong on a Saturday afternoon when I was in the city for a school event.

He left our town like he arrived, in the backseat of a luxury sedan surrounded by curious onlookers. Everyone pointed at him excitedly as he shut the car door. It was as if he was boarding a time machine.

When I got home that night, some neighborhood kids told me that Tiny had attempted to see me before he left. They thought that was quite a big deal. But I was sad to see him go. I sneaked down the alley to Auntie Yue's house and peeked in the window of Tiny's bedroom and found it dark.

When I turned back toward the alley, I heard the sound of a child crying. I knew it had to be the other Tiny, the fisherman's son. I later learned that he hadn't been there to see off the other Tiny either.

Tiny being picked up in the luxury car for his trip to Hong Kong was like an alien being scooped up by a flying saucer for his return to his home planet. His time in our small town had been nothing more than a dream. Tiny was an interloper from another time. I went back to being the Barefoot Immortal. It seemed like everyone forgot about

Tiny's appearance in our lives. Everything was as noisy and unsophisticated as ever.

The only person who seemed not to have forgotten was the Tiny who was left behind, the Tiny who still lived in the house across from mine.

He didn't have anyone to take him to the salon, so he tried to copy the other Tiny's Hong Kong style by himself, taking a pair of scissors to his own hair. He didn't have anyone to show off for, but he still harassed the migrant workers when he walked down the alley. He tried to get other people to join in. They weren't interested.

Since he wasn't in school anymore, there was only one fate possible for Tiny: he would become a fisherman. He tried to avoid it. He ended up getting in a fight with his father and running away from home. He showed up a month later, gaunt and hungry, and finally gave in. His only condition was that his father buy him a motorcycle. Tiny's father thought about it for a while and agreed, happy to see his son home again and ready to take up the family business.

Fishermen need to get up early to catch the tide. They have to head out around five or six in the morning. I heard the motorcycle roaring to life at dawn each day. He made a show of ripping down the alley at top speed, carrying his father on the back as they headed out to start spreading their nets. His two older brothers followed them, huffing and puffing on their bikes.

They finished each day at three or four in the afternoon. Tiny had been tanned a shade darker from working out on the deck. He dumped the catch at home, then tore off again. Nobody was sure exactly where he went, but I heard rumors that he liked to ride up the coastal highway going sixty miles an hour, whooping exuberantly.

When he went by my house, I noticed Tiny's hair getting longer and longer. I wondered to myself if he was trying to become the man that the other Tiny had wanted to be.


I hadn't expected Tiny to write to me after he went to Hong Kong. It was three years after he had left and I was getting ready to take the college entrance exam when I got his letter.

On the envelope, he had messily scrawled my name and the address of the middle school we had both gone to. Thankfully, the woman at the school in charge of receiving the mail sorted through thousands of past and present students to locate me. Maybe the Hong Kong postmark helped.

His penmanship hadn't improved, but I noticed that he had started using the traditional characters they used in Hong Kong:

> *Dear Blackie!*
> *Long time no see.*
> *Everything is good with me in Hong Kong. It's beautiful, lots of skyscrapers, come and see me if you have time.*

*I can't speak Cantonese, so it's hard to make friends.*
*Please write me when you can. I have nobody to talk to.*
  *I'm not living at that old address, so send it to my new*
*one. . . .*

Despite what he said, I knew he must not be having an easy time in Hong Kong. I couldn't help but picture him in a classroom full of kids with gleaming white teeth and crisp white shirts looking down on their classmate from a coastal backwater. I could only imagine what they must call him behind his back.

I suddenly felt very sad for him.

I took the letter and went to knock on the door of the house across the way. Wuxi showed me in and pointed me toward Tiny, who was bent over his guitar. Back then, the heroes in all of the Hong Kong TV series we watched played the guitar, so learning the guitar became a fad.

I took out the letter from Hong Kong.

Tiny looked at it for a moment. He seemed stunned. I held it out to him, but he didn't take it.

"He wrote you a letter?" Tiny asked.

I realized that Tiny had not written to Tiny after he had gone to Hong Kong.

He snatched the letter out of my hand and tossed it in the stove. That was how I ended up losing Tiny's Hong Kong address when my local Tiny let it burn.

I realized I had been too reckless.

I knew that I was forever cut off from both of them:

I couldn't write back to the Tiny in Hong Kong because I had let his address get burned up by the stove, and Tiny the fisherman's son thought I had showed him the letter to hurt him.

As we prepared to enter college, the teachers at our school began to sound more and more like someone trying to sell a pyramid scheme.

"Think about your future," they would say, "and stop fooling around. The day will come when you are in the city, and you can walk out your door and be surrounded by skyscrapers—that is the time to fool around! But you aren't there yet." They gave us examples of former students who had gotten into schools in Beijing and settled there. They could have added "and they lived happily ever after" to the end of these fables of academic success and big city life.

Nobody suspected that Beijing wasn't the final stop on an express train to happiness. The entire class began to resemble an expeditionary force preparing for its final campaign. Some students moved out of their houses to live in the school dormitories so they could avoid any distraction that would keep them from throwing themselves absolutely into their studies. They studied like monks entering into a meditation state. It was as if we had all boarded a spaceship, blasting off into the unknown in search of a more enlightened galaxy.

I was one of the students who moved into the dormitory ahead of the final academic sprint. When the exam was over, as soon as I went home, my mother told me to check on Tiny.

While riding up the coastal highway on his bike, he

had ended up crashing, being thrown off, and landing head first. It had happened two months earlier, while I was getting ready for my exam. He had been in critical condition, but by the time I saw him, he was well into a miraculous recovery.

I went over and found him in bed. The stitches had been taken out, but I could see that his forehead still had a dent in it. He was surprised to see me at first, but he smiled and said, "You know what I'm like. I banged myself up pretty good, but I made it out alive. Once I recovered from the accident, I was in the clear. I might have a couple of scars, but that's not going to hurt my reputation with the people I roll with."

Within a couple of months, I was receiving invitations from universities far from our hometown, and I made the decision to get out just like Tiny had once told me to. I went to say goodbye to him, but he had already left to go fishing. I noticed that he had left his motorcycle behind. He must have huffed and puffed out there on his bike just like his brothers used to.

He had become what he vowed he would never be: a hometown fisherman.


I rambled around for a while after graduating from university and ended up staying in Beijing. It was a city that could compare to the imaginary Hong Kong I still held in my head.

I had already realized that staying in Beijing wasn't

going to be the "happily ever after" to my story. It was just the beginning.

It was a massive city teeming with human life and driven by anxiety. Every time I descended into the crowded subway, I felt as if I had been swallowed whole by the city. I felt small and insignificant. Life back in my hometown seemed more complicated, more joyous. It was a more human place.

I even felt envious of Tiny the fisherman's son. I heard that he had gotten married, had a son, and had bought a piece of land to put a house on. Just like his father before him, he built what he could and left a yard in the back where he kept a dog.

Meanwhile I was nursing a perpetually sore neck, constantly stressed out about work, and when I went home, there was simply a void. The only consolation I had was that I was a writer working for a top international magazine, and my articles went around the world.

When my friends back home called me, they never suspected my life wasn't perfect. I played my role and they played theirs. But when I hung up the phone, the emptiness came rushing back in again.

One night I was going through the comments on my blog and saw one that read, "Is this really Blackie? This is Tiny. I'm in Hong Kong still. Can you give me a call?" He left his number.

I hesitated. I was scared to talk to him. I didn't want to know how he was—whether it was good or bad, it made me shudder to think about.

A few weeks went by, and I unexpectedly was sent to Hong Kong on business. I had written Tiny's number on a slip of paper before I left, but I still wasn't sure whether I would call him.

One day, with all my work done, alone in my empty hotel room, I finally worked up the nerve to dial the number.

"Hello?" a voice said, then in Cantonese, "Who's this?"

"Is this Tiny?" I asked.

"Huh?" I heard him say. He seemed shocked that I had called. "Blackie? Is that you? You're in Hong Kong? Finally we meet again, huh?"

He still remembered my voice. I knew then how lonely he must have been in Hong Kong.

Just like the first time Auntie Yue had invited me over, I was nervous about meeting Tiny. I was soaked in sweat as I sat in the diner waiting for him to arrive. I kept imagining what he would look like. Would he walk in with long hair blowing in the breeze? Would he be dressed as cool as ever, with an earring in his ear? He had complete freedom in Hong Kong to look and act however he wanted.

When Tiny came in, I knew right away that it was him. His body might have changed, but his face looked the same. His hair was cut short; he didn't have earrings in, but his ears still had piercing holes in them. He was well dressed, but the canvas sack he carried with him seemed out of place.

He smiled when he saw me, showing off tobacco-stained teeth. He enveloped me in a hug.

"Why didn't you write me back?" he asked.

I couldn't decide whether to tell him the truth. I decided it wasn't worth trying to explain.

As always, he was concerned about maintaining his reputation and impressing other people, so he invited me out to a fancy restaurant in the Mid-Levels where there was a beautiful nighttime view of Victoria Harbour.

We reminisced about the old days for a while, but eventually I couldn't hold back from asking him, "But how are you doing now?"

"Me? I'm working hard. Nothing like you, though. You made something of yourself!"

"Working hard at what?"

He held up his glass and paused, then chuckled to himself. He looked as if he had come to a momentous decision. He said, "I install anti-theft doors."

He explained that they were fortified steel doors with multiple locking mechanisms, and he made twelve thousand Hong Kong dollars a month.

I didn't know what to say. The silence between us grew thick. I started to panic.

Tiny made a valiant effort to get the conversation going. He told me the truth of his time in Hong Kong, about how his classmates had looked down on him, how he had never made any friends, how he was sick of the place, and how his parents' business had failed.

"You know what?" he said. "Now that I think about it, that little town was home, even if I looked down on it back then." He smiled at his own remark. "Even that's just wishful thinking. I don't have a home."

I knew there were things he wasn't telling me. Why didn't he have a home? What were his parents doing?

I realized that as honest as he had been, there were things he preferred to leave unsaid.

We finished eating around ten, and Tiny had to run to get the bus back home. I walked him to his stop.

There was a long line at the bus stop, with men in ties and cheap suits or the uniforms of appliance repair companies and women with the aprons they wore to work in hair salons. As he stepped on the bus, he paused and turned to ask me if I wanted to come with him. He figured since we had spent so much time apart, it might be nice to keep catching up. "We can stay up talking all night even!"

I thought for a moment and then followed him onto the bus.

The sign on top said the destination was Tin Shui Wai. I knew what that name meant to people in Hong Kong. As we wound our way between the skyscrapers, he told me what each one was. He told me more about his life over the past several years.

The bus left the urban core and headed out toward the edge of the city, where the lights become dimmer and farther between.

"We're almost there," Tiny said.

We drove out onto a long suspension bridge.

"This is the Tsing Yi Bridge, the longest suspension bridge in Asia. I cross it every day."

"Oh, really?" I asked, nodding politely.

He looked out at the bridge and then, as if talking to

himself, said, "I had been in Hong Kong for three years when my father found out he had cancer. It was nasopharyngeal carcinoma. There was no way for him to continue working. He went all over looking for a doctor and a hospital that could treat him. He was still hopeful at first, but my brother figured it was going to end badly. He took the money my parents had saved up and ran away. We had just sold our house so we could keep paying the medical bills, but one day I guess my father had enough. He drove out here on the bridge and jumped. Now, to make a living in this city, I have to pass by the spot every single day. . . ."

I was stunned. I didn't know what to say.

Tiny went on, still speaking as if only to himself: "This city is disgusting. As soon as my father got sick, his friends all disappeared. When he died, my mother and I were the only ones at his funeral."

He laughed softly to himself.

I opened my mouth but nothing came out. Tiny seemed to know how I felt.

"I'm fine," he said. "I'll get through it. You know, the newspapers here actually reported the case. We still have a copy of that day's paper. It was the top headline on the front page. Can you believe that?" He turned to me, and I saw that he was smiling even though his eyes were wet with tears.

The bus kept going. The bridge seemed never-ending. The lamps that lit the span rushed past the bus windows, illuminating the tired faces of the passengers, then fading, then illuminating them again.

Most of those riding the bus back home were tired enough to fall asleep. They had gotten up at seven in the morning to put on their makeup and their uniforms and take the bus into the city to jobs as maintenance men or dishwashers or appliance salesmen or hair stylists. When their workday ended, they rushed back to the bus to ride an hour or two back to the edge of town so that they could prepare for another day.

These people were as much a part of the city as anybody else. We had imagined Hong Kong as a paradise. These were people we assumed were living in a heaven on earth.

Tiny opened the bus window and let the wind rush in. I suddenly recalled the other Tiny, back at home in our small town. He had started riding his motorcycle again, I had heard.

While we were on the bus, he would be getting the nets ready for the next day, and then he would jump on his motorcycle and roar back home up the levee. He had a house and a wife and a son. He had a black dog that rushed out into the alley at the sound of his motorcycle and greeted him with a wagging tail.

# 8

# Wenzhan

I fell ill around the time I was eleven.

It wasn't a serious illness, but I lost all inclination to speak or eat, and I wanted to isolate myself. When he heard my symptoms, the doctor I went to see in my small town was disdainful, or perhaps he simply couldn't wrap his head around that kind of illness. It wasn't a time of excess, and patience wasn't a luxury anyone could spare. My illness was considered no better than an indulgence.

"Leave him alone for a while," the doctor said. "He'll feel better soon."

He was the same doctor who had treated my cat, and he had also looked after the cow my nana had raised. He prescribed the same medicine to the cat and the cow, only modifying the dosage. My cat died that same night, but the cow managed to hang on for a month. When it looked like the end was near for Nana's cow, she sent for the butcher. "If a cow dies on its own, you can't eat the meat." That was the reason my nana sent for the butcher instead of the doctor.

She went tottering around on her formerly bound feet, delivering cuts of meat in a basket to relatives and friends. She made sure she went to see the doctor, too. He didn't wait for her to say anything, but immediately said, "You should thank me. If it wasn't for me, that cow wouldn't have lived a whole month longer."

When my mother heard the doctor's prescription for me, she went to my father and told him, "I think it's more serious, but the doctor doesn't have a solution. We have to do something for him."

My father was a real man, and to him that meant not spending a lot of time pondering complex solutions to things. What made my father feel good was surrounding himself with friends, so he decided the same prescription might work for me: "He needs some kids his age to play with. Find someone for him."

My mother brought Wenzhan over the next day.

That was the first time we met.


My mother hadn't devoted much time to vetting Wenzhan.

Back then, the adults in our town all had a special talent, which was being able to eat with a bowl of rice in one hand and a small dish balanced on the wrist where they put a few pieces of pickled mustard or some meat. That was so they could move around while eating, the women getting together to gossip about this and that, and the men gathering in a corner to crouch down and talk about their own topics.

The Saturday I met Wenzhan, my mother took her

lunch and went over to one of our neighbors' homes. She came back with Wenzhan. His house was behind ours. He was a year older than me, and he was also—my mother emphasized this point—"a pretty good student."

I don't remember how his face looked looming over me. I only remember saying, "Oh," covering my eyes with the back of my hand, and going back to sleep. During that time, I used to nap after meals. When I woke up, I would stare blankly at the wall until it was time to eat again, and then I would go back to sleep.

My indifference didn't deter Wenzhan. I have a memory of him looking me over and then turning to examine the rest of the room before sitting calmly at the foot of my bed. There was something ritualistic about his vigil. He looked like a holy man convinced that the first task on his spiritual quest was to enlighten or save me.

He prodded me and said, "Get up. Let's chat."

"I don't want to," I said.

"We might as well. You want to spend the rest of your life in bed?"

I base this only on my own observations, but I've noticed that when kids reach the age of twelve or thirteen, words like "life" and "dreams" enter their vocabulary in a major way. When I encountered these significant terms, I felt a subconscious anxiety rising. When Wenzhan asked me that question, it had the desired effect. "There's nothing to talk about," I said. "There's no point hanging around here bothering me. I'm not interested. I'm not interested in anything."

"That's exactly why I want to talk to you," Wenzhan

said. "I'm here to tell you: we have an opportunity to follow our dreams. You can leave all of this behind."

That made me sit up. He had managed to put his finger on exactly the point that had been bothering me. I thought it might be because he suffered from the same problem. I was growing up in a town without a single paved street, just packed dirt roads and cobblestone alleys, and all of those unpaved lanes were lined with the same chaotic cityscape. Around that time I had started to ponder what life held in store for me. When I imagined that I would one day become like all the other adults I knew, I felt a petrifying hopelessness.

Back then, I couldn't conceive of my small town as anything but dull, so I imagined my future in that town would be equally dull. But what had made me sit up in bed was Wenzhan's sincerity. When he opened his arms to punctuate his words, perhaps he imagined himself as an eagle soaring overhead—as skinny as he was, he looked more like a clothes drying rack hung with wet laundry.

"So," he went on, "we have to build a life for ourselves." Every word of that speech was carved into my memory. At the time, it impressed me that there was a person not only making such a bold statement but also taking it completely seriously.

After he finished delivering his speech, my mind went blank for a few seconds, and I had a vision of a vast blank space like a barren plain, like the open ocean, like the boundless sky. . . .

I looked at him, suddenly feeling a bit light-headed. I thought for a while, then said, "I have to sleep. Come back tomorrow. We can talk."

As he left, I managed to focus my eyes enough to get a better look at him, and I realized he had a cleft lip.

I went to see him the next day.

After his speech, I had begun to once again pay attention to the world around me. I made a careful survey of Wenzhan, too, noting the ill-fitting suit pants and baggy white shirt he wore, both clearly castoffs from an older sibling.

His thin chest looked like a washboard, but he insisted on keeping the top three buttons of the shirt undone. Maybe, I thought, he liked the way it moved in the breeze. Maybe it felt like he was floating.

What really made an impression, though, was his cleft lip, which split his upper lip and locked his mouth at a particular angle.

In my childhood, the evil—even if it was subconscious—that children most commonly perpetrated was attacking the physical defects of their peers. Children quickly realize their own defects and learn to hide them, always fearing that they will be uncovered. That fear of exposure drives them into a dead end. I had seen it myself many times: kids with some obvious physical defect being laughed at, then banished to the margins of the in-group. Those kids gave up on their dreams. They were destined to never enjoy the benefits of their peers. Their lives would forever be marred by that persecution.

Wenzhan was the only one who had overcome this pattern. I couldn't help but admire him.

When I arrived at his house, I realized that I was only one of many neighborhood kids who seemed to gather there every Sunday. Nearly half of my younger neighbors were scattered around the living room as if waiting for Wenzhan to grant them an audience.

On Wenzhan's rounds of our neighborhood, he was always looking for other kids to talk to. He invited them to his house and waited for them to gather at the appointed time. When the group had assembled, he would address them: "In a little while, we're going down to the beach to dig clams." He put two kids in charge of getting some shovels, assigned two others to find a set of scales so they could weigh out the clams they harvested before selling them, and sent two others to get a pair of shoulder poles. . . . Everyone was organized into regiments that set out from Wenzhan's house. On the way, he kept his team entertained with a long talk that included a legend about the white-snake fairy who he claimed lived in the forest near the beach, as well as a brief history of our own town.

None of the activities were particularly unusual, but the way the kids listened to Wenzhan's directions was truly remarkable. These were kids who were thirsting for freedom, and it was no easy thing for one of their peers to lead them. I realized, however, that some of the kids were not particularly interested and seemed to be only half-heartedly tagging along.

Even if the enthusiasm wasn't unanimous, when I watched him loftily proclaim the day's schedule, with his cleft lip giving him a peculiar speech impediment, I wondered how he got so many of the neighborhood kids to follow him. I couldn't figure out how he had managed to install himself as the leader of these kids. They could have made fun of him or revolted against his leadership, but they didn't.

The reason was that he was already operating on a higher plane than these kids were, but I only realized that later. I know it's a simplistic explanation, but it's the only thing that explains his stubborn commitment to his project.

I joined the so-called Wenzhan Battalion, too (it was later renamed the Barefoot Army), and I learned Wenzhan was planning a project that would be even bigger than his current efforts.

Wenzhan's troops were on a strict schedule. They got together every weekday afternoon at 4:30, when school let out, until 6:00, when it was time to head home for dinner; on weekends, they spent all day together.

On Saturday and Sunday, Wenzhan's troops went out on exercises, which mostly involved roasting sweet potatoes, swimming, digging clams, and things like that. Through the week, they did their homework together, then started playing board games like Monopoly and checkers, battle chess, *xiangqi*, and *weiqi*. I don't know why he had so many board games at his place, but he had nearly everything we could have wanted to play.

The games themselves weren't the real attraction—it was chatting and talking trash while playing. Talk often turned to vague boasting about the big project Wenzhan had planned.

"He'll be just as powerful as President Zhang!" one of the kids said.

"Maybe," another said, "but if he can pull it off, he'll go down in history like Chairman Mao."

I asked for details, trying to figure out exactly what Wenzhan was planning.

"You wouldn't even get it," one of the kids said to me disdainfully. "It's going to be massive."

Finally I couldn't stand it, and when everyone else had left for the day, I went to ask Wenzhan. "Everyone is talking about this project," I started cautiously, "but what is it exactly?"

When he smiled, his cleft lip blanched pale and he looked even stranger. "You want to see it?" he asked me.

I nodded.

"I haven't shown them yet," he said, leading me toward his room, "but I can let you see it."

Wenzhan shared a room with his older brother, and I could tell their relationship was not harmonious by the stark divide between the two sides of the room.

He pulled a beige suitcase from under his bed. I guessed that it must have come from his mother's family when she married into a new household. He opened the suitcase, and I saw that it was filled with stacks of paper covering a layer of books.

He took the paper out sheet by sheet and stacked it up on the floor. "Look at this," he said in a low voice. "For each year in Chinese history, I wrote down the major events, then made my own attempt at an explanation. . . . I've been working on this since I was nine years old. Every day after dinner, I come back to it. I figure if I can get through a millennium before I'm eighteen, I'll consider myself a success." His face had flushed a deep crimson, and I imagined I could see the blood vessels throbbing under his cheeks.

I felt a strange sensation, as if there was steam rising from my head and all of the pores in my skin had opened up. I looked at him with wide eyes. Whether he finished it or not, I thought he was already amazing.

After Wenzhan showed me what he was working on, I started going to his house every day. I dutifully played board games alongside the other kids, but I was just biding my time before asking about the project. "Are you going to be working on it today?" I would ask him.

He always smiled serenely, and when he looked up at me, I felt like there was some holy gleam in his eyes. I felt as if I were witnessing a momentous project being shepherded into the light.

I had always been a good student, but Wenzhan's project had given me a sort of desperation to succeed at school.

Even though I easily managed to finish at the top of my class, it was no longer enough for me. I felt a constant anxiety. Sometimes I felt like I couldn't catch my breath. I wanted to keep pace with Wenzhan.

I wanted to take every opportunity to talk to Wenzhan.

At first he kept telling me not to worry, that he would wait until I finished first in my class again to talk to me seriously. When I got my exam scores, I went to see him again. I got some satisfaction out of his obvious surprise at my academic success. I asked him, "What should I do now?"

"You have to think about the kind of life you want for yourself, then figure out a plan to accomplish it." That was all he said. Among the neighborhood kids, Wenzhan seemed to think I was the only one qualified to enter into that sort of metaphysical dialogue with him.

Maybe Wenzhan had kept everything bottled up for too long and he was waiting for the chance to lay it out for someone, because that afternoon he went a step further. "Take me, for example," he said. "I want to move to a big city, so I want to get into university or maybe a highly rated technical school. Getting into a top high school and then into university wouldn't be an issue, but I have to think about the cost. My parents are poor. I think a technical school would be the best place for me. But I have to think about my test scores. They can't go too high or too low, and I think I've finally managed to figure out how to control that. But moving to the city is only the first step. Once I get there, I don't want to leave, so I'll need to find some way to make myself stand out. That's why I want to develop my leadership skills, so that maybe someday I can lead the student union. That's a great way to start networking and get noticed by the right people."

I suddenly figured out another piece of the puzzle. "All those group activities you put us through are leadership training?" I asked.

Wenzhan nodded proudly. "And my outline of Chinese history is in preparation for writing the essay portion of the high school entrance exam. I should be able to get a decent score. Later on, though, I heard that the civil service exam puts a lot of weight on examples from history, so I figured I'd be able to score some extra points there, too."

It took my breath away. I felt like I had been living my life all wrong. I had been far too naive. "I, too, desire a life like that," I said. "How would I accomplish this?" Shock and awe had rendered me temporarily verbose.

"You have to find your own route," Wenzhan said calmly. "I'll wait for you in the city. I believe in you." He patted my shoulder softly. We looked like two generals on one of those TV shows about fighting the Japanese. That must have been where he learned the move.

Wenzhan probably didn't realize what his speech had done to me. I was completely destroyed. For the rest of summer vacation, I was thrown into an abyss of self-doubt.

When I was playing with my friends, I asked myself, "What's the point?" When I thought of finishing at the top of my class, I asked myself, "What's the point?" My mother sent me off to visit my grandparents once a week, and I asked myself, "What's the point?" I couldn't figure out what the point of any of it was—what was the point if it wasn't being done with a goal in mind?

I didn't think anybody had the answer except for Wenzhan.

That summer vacation, Wenzhan seemed to be attempting to restructure his plan. He kept his battalion of kids drilling, but he reduced the schedule so that they only met on Sunday afternoons. On that single afternoon, Wenzhan tried out experimental exercises with his forces, and the rest of the time he stayed shut up in his room.

My depression sent me in search of him. He tried to send me away. "You have to find your own path," he said. "I can't help you plan your own life."

I began to suffer from insomnia. I stayed up all night trying to make my way through Schopenhauer, Nietzsche, and Kant. The way my mother remembered it, I spent that summer vacation walking around in a daze.

Anyone could tell at a glance that my illness had returned and was worse than before. My mother understood that only Wenzhan could help me.

Wenzhan finally relented and agreed to see me again.

He walked into my room looking irritable. "Do you know what you've done? I planned to get so much done this summer, but because you kept bothering me, I'm only 80 percent finished. I'm getting ready for high school, and this is a big deal for me. You have to promise to leave me alone."

I nodded.

"What you need to know is that it's completely normal not to have a goal. Very few young people figure out what their life is going to be like. You need to take it as it comes. That's the best thing for you to do right now."

"How come you figured it out already?" I asked.

Maybe that question touched something deep inside him, because he suddenly opened his eyes wide and looked as if he had come to some grand conclusion. Wenzhan turned to me and said very seriously, "It's because I have talent."

He paused and seemed to remember his reason for coming. "I think you have talent, too," he said, "but you need to stop worrying so much. Take things as they come. Do the best you can. You'll get your answer eventually."

"Really?"

"Really."

I started to cry. I hadn't expected that.


After summer vacation, Wenzhan went on to junior high school. As he told it, he was engaging in the first key battle of his life. Around that time, a new policy had been announced that pushed top-rated technical schools to only accept outstanding students, so Wenzhan had to make sure his exam scores stayed high. I knew how hard it would be for him.

I started trying to avoid him. I felt coarse and boorish in his eyes. The old anxiety rose up again.

But when we ran into each other, he was unexpectedly friendly and invited me to walk with him. He updated me on his plans. "We just did the test for our last unit," he said. "I got a 90 last time, right as I had planned, and this time I only got one more point than I had planned on, so I can tell I'm getting better at controlling my grades."

All I could do was smile.

"What about you?" he asked.

"I don't know. I'm just trying to take it as it comes. I'll worry about the big stuff when it comes."

"Don't worry," he said, encouragingly. "When the time comes, you'll figure it out."

I wasn't the only one who felt abandoned by Wenzhan. Maybe his schedule was too tight or maybe it was because he no longer needed to sharpen his leadership skills, but he had reduced his time with his neighborhood battalion to an hour on Saturday.

They came to me to ask what was going on.

"Maybe he's being selfish," I said. "Maybe he decided that he doesn't need us anymore." Even I was stunned by what I had said. I realized that I had fallen to some extent under Wenzhan's spell. I realized that I had begun to hate Wenzhan.

I wondered to myself: What would failure look like for Wenzhan?

I didn't expect to get my answer so quickly. My mother was my source for insider information on Wenzhan, and one day she came home with the news that the stress of his exams was giving him headaches. His test scores had been steadily declining, he couldn't sleep, and his hair had begun to come out in clumps. "His parents are worried about him," my mother said. "You should go over to see him. Bring some of your other friends, too."

"He doesn't need us," I said. "There's nothing we can do for him. He can look after himself." When I said Wenzhan didn't need us, maybe I was speaking out of anger, but it was true: there was no longer anything we could do for him.

One day I decided to talk to him on the way to school.

He was clearly in a sensitive state. When I tried to comfort him, he cut me off, saying, "Oh, so you think you're going to give me guidance now?"

Perhaps he was going for a cold and condescending tone, but the tension in his voice and his cleft lip made it come out in a nasal honk.

Legend had it that our town in southern Fujian was first settled during the Jin Dynasty, a kingdom that reunified China after the Three Kingdoms period. Some traditions were said to date back to those times, including a ceremony for outstanding scholars held on the day of the Lantern Festival. In modern times, it was the town's Education Committee that handed out awards recognizing top students at local schools.

In the years before that, Wenzhan had always finished first among his age group. I did well, but there was always a battle among the top three students my age, all of us fighting for the top slot. With my depression and anxiety, I had slipped to sixth place and didn't even want to bother going to accept my award. My mother encouraged me to go, though, saying, "I'll let you keep the award money." I figured I could buy two comic books with the fifty yuan I would receive, so I worked up the nerve and went to the ceremony.

The awards ceremony still followed some tenets of the ancient system. It began with distinguished local scholars reading out the list of donors. They read the names in a sonorous, self-satisfied tone, their heads wobbling. After that, they began, in the same tone, to read the list of award recipients. They started out with the youngest students, slowly working their way up to the oldest, with the award bonuses increasing with age.

I used to love the cadence and tone with which the distinguished gentlemen read the names. I felt a sense of importance in being included on their list. But that day I was too anxious to enjoy it. I paced nervously, watching the students as they were called on stage to receive their award. When they came to Wenzhan's age group, I was surprised not to hear his name called.

My pulse began to thud. I ran home as fast as I could, carrying my award money with me. When I got there, I breathlessly informed my mother what had happened: "Wenzhan didn't get called. He didn't make the list. Maybe he didn't do well on his exams. He failed!"

"What do you mean?" my mother demanded. "You're talking about Wenzhan! It's impossible."

Word of Wenzhan's absence from the list of outstanding students began to circulate among the neighborhood kids.

Everyone came to the same conclusion: it was impossible that Wenzhan could have failed his exams, so there must have been some sort of clerical oversight that made him ineligible.

We went looking for Wenzhan, hoping he could confirm our theory, but he spent the winter break in self-imposed confinement.

In the past, Wenzhan had given his parents strict orders that they were to keep an open-door policy, so we never had any trouble finding him. But the door to his house was shut tight all winter break. We stood outside, beating on the door and yelling for him to come out, and Wenzhan's mother came out to inform us of her son's new orders: "He's studying. The high school entrance exams are coming up. He doesn't have time to play."

The Wenzhan Battalion slowly dissolved. New groups were formed, with pairs and trios breaking off. I tried to keep myself separate from whatever mischief they were getting up to. I decided I was better off staying home. When I got bored, I started writing stories. When I had finished writing, I read the stories to myself.

My mother was worried about me. I overheard her saying to someone, "Maybe he's burned out from all his homework." And then she turned to her real concern: "Just look at what happened to that neighbor boy, Wenzhan. Even he turned into a weirdo."

With the fear of burnout looming, her solution to my problem was to keep me out of school for half a semester and send me to Ningbo, where my father was working on the boats.

Back then, Ningbo seemed like a giant metropolis compared to my small town. I was staying in a hotel in the Old Bund neighborhood, the area of the port city that had first been opened up to foreign merchants. I met city kids and got my first taste of city air. I didn't carry much away from Ningbo when I left, but I managed to leave behind plenty of baggage brought from home.

When I finally returned home, it was the eve of final exams, and the junior high school students were preparing to take the test that would decide which high school they would attend.

I started to worry about Wenzhan again. I was trying to catch up on the schoolwork I had missed, but I made time to stop by his house. I wanted to give him the postcard I had bought for him in Ningbo. I thought this might have a calming effect on him and maybe encourage him to follow his dream of leaving our small town for the big city.

The door to his house was still shut.

Eventually, the time for the high school entrance exams passed, and it was time for me to go through my personal torture, taking my own final exams. After that, it was summer vacation.

After I returned from Ningbo, my home became a place for neighborhood kids to congregate. They wanted to see all the things I had brought back with me and ask about life in the big city.

At first, I appreciated the aura of sophistication that my trip had granted me, but I eventually got tired of answering the same questions. I couldn't help but think, what's the point of fawning over someone just because they had visited a city? I went to see Wenzhan, but the door was still tightly shut.

Halfway through summer vacation, I lost all patience with questions about the city. I drove away my interrogators and shut myself up in my room. I started trying to come up with stories again.

One afternoon while I was taking a nap, I heard my mother talking to someone in the other room. I didn't know whom she was talking to, but the voice seemed unusually forceful. I was curious enough to get out of bed and take a look. My mother was talking to Wenzhan.

He walked into the room and threw up his hands. "I did it," he said. "I got into a vocational school in Fuzhou. I barely made the cut. I showed them, though—everyone who ever doubted me."

I thought he was being a bit extreme, but I was still excited for him. I didn't care that he was moving to the city or anything like that; I was just happy that he had come back to life.

He still wanted to plan his future life, and he was looking forward to life in the big city. "Will you come with me to the Neighborhood Committee?" he asked me, suddenly very solemn. "I have to get my residency transferred from here to Fuzhou."

I told him I'd go with him. He seemed to want to comfort me because I had been worried about him since he had been left off the list of outstanding students. "After I get to Fuzhou," he said, "I'm going to write to you every week. I'll tell you all about my life. I know you'll get to the city someday, too."

I knew I should nod happily even if I didn't really feel it.

Wenzhan prepared to go off to the city, climbing aboard a tractor driven by a friend of his father's, and he once again provided an example to his peers. His parents wept with gratitude imagining their son's bright future, and his father's estranged elder brother arrived with his whole family, congratulating his nephew and saying, "I know you'll be successful, but I want you to remember to do your best to look after my kids—they're your cousins."

Wenzhan already looked like a returning hero, even though he had not yet left. He said a special goodbye to everyone who arrived to see him off.

Just before the tractor left, he turned to me and shouted, "I'll be waiting for you, Blackie!"

I waved to him as the tractor pulled away. I felt proud that Wenzhan still held out hope that we would someday reunite in the big city.

Wenzhan was true to his word, and his first letter arrived a week after he had left.

He had carefully selected a Fuzhou commemorative envelope and stamp and wrote the letter on stationery with his school letterhead at the top.

He wrote to me about his first impressions of the city and his own plans. He told me that his first goal was to make a survey of the city, discovering how "the city flows and grows" by tracing the main roads of Fuzhou, then heading off onto secondary streets.

In Wenzhan's next letter, he told me that he was about to embark on a week of military training. He told me that it would test his will. He considered it a "very worthwhile" form of "intelligence." He told me that among his personal strengths were willpower and determination, so he thought it would be a good way to win the respect of his classmates.

The third letter didn't come as promptly as the first two. I decided it must be because of his military training. When the letter finally came, he sounded exhausted. He didn't say anything in particular about the military training. Instead he said, "My cleft lip has become the focus of some of my more vulgar classmates' cruel attacks. This is what they have resorted to, since they realize they cannot beat me any other way. I refuse to stoop to their level. If I hold myself above them, I know they will one day learn to fear and maybe even revere me."

There was no fourth letter.

I started to get a bit worried after a couple of weeks went by. I decided to go around to his house to see if his family knew anything. His older brother answered the door. While Wenzhan was following his dreams in the city, his brother had dropped out of school. He always seemed like the flip side of Wenzhan. He had dropped out without making any plans and wasn't able to find a job, so he was living off his parents.

"Do you have any idea how Wenzhan's doing in Fuzhou?" I asked him. "I was expecting a letter from him. I was worried he might have gotten in trouble."

"I don't talk to him," he said. "You know how he is—he doesn't want to hear from me. I heard he's having a hard time, though. They keep making fun of his cleft lip. He got in a fight with someone. The school wanted my parents to go in and meet with them, but they don't want to pay for the ticket."

I rushed home to write a letter to Wenzhan. I tried to find a tactful way to ask what was going on and asked vaguely whether he had run into any particular challenges during his time at school. I figured he could accept that question.

I got a reply three weeks later. It was very brief: "Don't worry about me. I've run into some challenges, but that was accounted for in my plan. I should be able to put them to rest before the end of the semester. I may not have time to write you often, but I look forward to seeing you during summer vacation."

Wenzhan came home before the start of vacation, though. He told me his course work had been too basic, so he decided to take some time off.

All the former members of his Wenzhan Battalion arrived to pay their respects. They wanted to hear about life outside our small town. Wenzhan was happy to oblige at first, and he would spin vivid stories of life in the big city. After a week went by, he was once again shut up inside his house.

Wenzhan's mother told the kids who knocked at the door, "Wenzhan doesn't think it's worthwhile to spend all day talking to you. He wants to be alone. He's working on something big."

Even if there was nobody else he could talk to, I figured he might still think I was worth his time.

When all the neighborhood kids gave up on Wenzhan, I went and knocked at his door. I didn't want to ask him about life in Fuzhou. I felt like something unusual was happening with him, and I wanted to know what it was. I thought maybe he had fallen sick with the same illness that once kept me in my bed.

Wenzhan was still willing to see me, unlike the other kids. He tried to dominate the conversation, but he seemed out of breath. A skinny teenager panting as he talked, he seemed to me to be holding back something big.

I planned out the conversation in advance. I decided I would ask him for advice, since I knew that would put him at ease. I tried to make conversation about my own high school entrance exam, which was coming up next year, and the trials I was going through as I prepared to take it. I told him that my parents wanted me to go to a teacher training vocational school and get a job teaching elementary school. My parents told me that it would be a "simple, comfortable life." All I wanted to do was go to high school, then on to university, so that I could experience life beyond our small town.

Just as I had planned, Wenzhan took the bait and started giving me suggestions. He warned me to stay away from teacher training. "A small town like this sucks the life out of you," he said. He thought it would be better for me to aim for university and start preparing for life beyond the small town. "When you move to the city, you'll realize how low and coarse the people here are. You'll end up hating this place. This is where you were raised, but all it does is drag you down." He spoke very seriously.

I never worked up the nerve to ask him about his trouble in Fuzhou. I was going to ask how to deal with people making fun of you. To tell you the truth, from that day on, I made a clean break with Wenzhan. He was like a drowning man, and I was worried that if I got too close to him, he would pull me under with him.

When winter vacation came around again, I went to the ceremony to hear the men reading in their solemn tone the list of students with hopeful futures. As they always did, they read off the names of all the students who had tested into high school or vocational schools and presented them with awards. Wenzhan's name had been written on a banner that hung on the doorway to the hall. He never showed up, though.

Once again, people were nervous and curious about Wenzhan, but I didn't bother stopping by to see him.

Whatever was going on with him, whether it was the same illness that had laid me low before or something else, I was worried that it might be contagious.

I was worried that, like Wenzhan, I would grow to hate the place that had formed me and resent the people who had raised me.

He left later that year, but I wasn't sure where he was going. When summer vacation came around again, he still hadn't returned, but I didn't even notice. Even if we had grown up only a couple of houses apart, we were already living in different worlds.

When I saw his mother, she told me, "Wenzhan told me he wants to stay in the city. That's what he's working on doing. He told me he hopes he never has to come back here."

It's sometimes the case that the more you try to reject someone or someplace, the tighter and more inextricably you become perversely bound to it. You fight so hard to escape what it is you resent and are disgusted by, you find yourself exhausted, sinking even deeper into it. I was trying to understand what drove Wenzhan. I tried to imagine what kind of life he led in the city.

By my third year of high school, Wenzhan was still completely absent from my life. When I was choosing possible schools ahead of my university entrance exam, I decided I wanted to see Wenzhan again. I wasn't sure how I felt about him. I thought maybe he represented the type of person who came from a small town like ours. Maybe there was something pure about his ambition. Maybe I carried the same thing with me, too. Maybe I had a part of what drove Wenzhan.

Wenzhan stayed away from our small town. He called once a year, when everyone was celebrating the New Year. All he had to tell his parents was that he was chasing his dreams. His parents still expected him to someday return home triumphantly. Meanwhile, Wenzhan's older brother was "idle," as Wenzhan might say. He lived off his parents for a while, then got married young. He was married before his twentieth birthday and had a kid of his own shortly afterward. He was one of the "useless fathers" that Wenzhan hated, but he made a comfortable life for himself in our hometown.

When I went off to university and started my "life in the city," I met plenty of people who reminded me of Wenzhan. They would talk about their plans for the future, too. Their early academic success had given them confidence, and they expected to rocket out of elementary and middle school into a bright future. I could always detect the faint traces of rural upbringing on them, as if the aroma of their native soil clung to them. They were never as sophisticated as their city cousins, but they were honest and straightforward. That meant nobody ever noticed how ambitious and shrewd they were—just as ambitious and shrewd as anyone raised in the big city. After I got to the city, many of my friends fell in that category. I treated them like a local delicacy added to a big city banquet. We made friends, but I knew I wasn't quite like them. I wasn't the type of person who could see the big picture. I preferred to take things as they came, incrementally working toward a better life. I didn't want to transform my life, but instead slowly, piece by piece, turn it into a life worth living.

Those Wenzhan types, whenever they got excited, started to unconsciously raise their voices until they were almost shouting. Wenzhan had been the same. They reminded me of my childhood friend with his cleft lip. When I was swallowed up in a crowd in the big city, I often found myself suddenly wondering how Wenzhan was getting by.

After university, I got a job as a reporter. I couldn't think of anything more wonderful than being given the job of discovering what made individuals special. The higher I climbed in the profession, the bigger the platform I had, and the more freedom I had to meet people. I became completely swept up in it all and, without really meaning to, ended up in Beijing.

When people are left alone, they go back to being what they have always been. When I settled in Beijing, the first thing I did was to go out to Jingshan Park and buy a ticket to go up the hill that overlooks the city. As I made my way to the top, I tried to imagine what Wenzhan would have been thinking if he were here in my place. Maybe he would be imagining himself as the conquering hero, the city spread out below him just as his future was. I was more ambivalent:

I knew I would enjoy having a bigger platform at a job in Beijing, but I wondered if I would get any real satisfaction out of life in the big city.

When I got to the highest point in the park, I had the urge to call Wenzhan. I had gotten his number on my last trip home. His mother always made sure she came to see me during the New Year break to give me Wenzhan's latest contact information. She said, "You should give him a call if you've got the time." I knew Wenzhan's mother was worried about her son, even though she wouldn't voice her concerns. I think she thought if she said it out loud, it might just manifest her darkest fears.

The call went through. Wenzhan answered: "Talk to me, brother! Who's there?" I noticed that the speech impediment from his cleft lip seemed to be gone. He seemed to have overcome his disability again.

I was on the verge of speaking, but something made me hang up instead. There was something about the way he answered that put me off. He sounded like some oily businessman. I didn't know what to say to the new Wenzhan.

Maybe he knew that I had asked his mother about him, or maybe he just guessed it was me calling, but a week after the aborted phone call, I got a letter from Wenzhan, sent to the address I had put on my blog.

He enthusiastically praised what he called my "accomplishments." He went on to write, "You're the only one of us from back home who ended up in Beijing. I hear you're working for a big company, too." He mentioned that he had seen some of my articles and offered his own critique. He told me he was preparing for a major project that would finally show everyone who had ever looked down on him. When he had finished this latest project, he would finally be able to hold his head high.

I thought for a long time about what to say and finally wrote, "Nobody looks down on you. It's been a long time since they've seen you at all. You should go back for the New Year break. We can get everyone together again, just like the old days."

Until I left to work in the city, I didn't realize how much I would miss my hometown. After I got settled in Beijing and had the financial wherewithal, I tried to get as much time off work as I could so that I could go back to my hometown for the New Year holiday and other local festivals. The road by my house had already been paved a few times since I had left. The old neighborhood had changed countless times; it was no longer a uniform city-scape of stone and brick. My own house had been reno-vated and now stood at four stories. I stayed on the top floor, and I could see Wenzhan's room from the balcony. Over the years, Wenzhan's house had stayed the same. On those trips home, I often sat at my desk and looked over at the house and Wenzhan's darkened room.

Wenzhan didn't reply to my letter. He didn't return home for the New Year holiday. I didn't expect him to contact me again either. But I decided to reconnect with some of my other former playmates. I decided it would be a good idea to interview them.

Some of them had already gotten married and had kids of their own. One of them told me about running a shop at the night market. A few others told me about working as fishermen, and they took a self-conscious step back, asking if I could smell it on them. One had opened a clothing factory and was making a decent living. He took me out for dinner and bragged about the age of the mao-tai he was forcing me to drink. He pulled me close to him and said passionately, "We're still brothers, right? If you don't look down on me for staying here, I won't look down on you for being broke. Let's have another drink, huh?"

I realized that my proposal to Wenzhan to get the old gang back together was hopelessly naive. Everyone had moved on. They were leading their own lives, living in their own worlds. It was hard to get people from different walks of life together, even if they had once been friends. I knew the next time they would come back together would be many years from then, when old age had wiped out all the differences between them. When you're old, it seems to wipe clean all other identities.

Shortly after I got back to Beijing, my mother called to tell me that Wenzhan's father had died of a stroke. "Wenzhan came back for the funeral," she said, "and I didn't even recognize him. He looked frail and his skin was so dark, his hair was falling out, and he didn't want to talk to anyone."

A month after that, my mother called again to say that Wenzhan had gotten a job in our hometown. "His mother wanted him to stay," my mother told me, "or that's what I heard at least. She got him a job at the town broadcasting station. He's going to be an electrician, but they're going to let him edit some stuff, too."

When I heard Wenzhan was back for good, I started trying to come up with some excuse to head home. I knew I couldn't tell my boss—or my mother either—that I was going home just to see a childhood friend.

The more I scrambled for a reason to go home, the more hopeless I became. I ended up delaying the trip for a whole year, preparing to head back for the New Year holiday.

The month before I was set to leave, I started to try to imagine what it would be like to see Wenzhan again. I tried to decide whether I would give him a polite handshake or pull him in for a hug, like we would have done back when we were still close friends.

I knew it wouldn't be easy, since it had been more than ten years since we had last seen each other. They say that all of the cells in your body are completely replaced every ten years, so that meant we were both basically new people.

I left Beijing for my hometown as early as I could, but I didn't go directly to see Wenzhan. The way I thought, we lived close enough together that I would eventually run into him. I thought that was a better idea than going up and knocking on his door.

Just as I had expected, a few days after returning home, I caught sight of him coming up the alley. I figured he must be heading home. I called out, "Wenzhan!" I waved excitedly, and he looked up and seemed to see me, but he just kept going, turning into a smaller lane that led off the alley.

I asked my mother what time Wenzhan got off work, then, saying I was going "out for a stroll," went to stake out the alley. He appeared right on schedule, and we repeated the same procedure, me waving to him and him glancing up and then turning down the lane.

I knew Wenzhan was avoiding me, but I wasn't sure why.

With the end of the holiday quickly approaching, I knew I would have to go knock on his door.

His house was only about fifty or sixty feet from mine, a right turn and a short walk down the alley. His door was still the same; the sounds of my knuckles on it sounded the same, too. "Is Wenzhan home?" I called.

"Who's there?" Wenzhan's mother said from the other side of the door.

"It's me. I came to see Wenzhan."

The door swung open. Wenzhan's mother smiled warmly. "He's in his room," she said. "You can find your way."

Of course I could.

Although I hadn't been inside his house in more than a decade, it seemed as if nothing had changed. The house matched the blurry snapshot saved in my memory, but when I focused on the scene, I started to see that it wasn't quite as I had remembered. It seemed smaller, I thought. The walls were mottled, too, everything seemed worn out, and there was a moldy smell in the air.

When I got to Wenzhan's bedroom, I found the door shut. I knocked and Wenzhan opened it.

He was just as my mother had described: skinny, tanned dark, with his hair thinning. Something else had changed in him, though, something below the surface. . . . He was hunched over, and his eyes were slits, as if he was both weary and on his guard. His cold expression did not look like studied indifference but actual apathy.

"It's been a long time, Wenzhan," I said. I tried to talk to him as if no more time had passed than the week or two we might have spent apart as children.

He seemed surprised to see me. He stared back at me.

I was stunned silent for a moment, too. I wondered whether I should move in to hug him, but I could tell from his expression and his attitude that this wasn't the same Wenzhan I had known as a child. It was as if his life had whittled him down into something lesser. I could still detect hints of the old Wenzhan here and there: the tilt of his eyebrows, something lingering on his face—it was still him somewhere inside that body.

Wenzhan made the first move for me. He didn't shake my hand or embrace me but pointed at a chair. "Take a seat," he said coldly.

It was still light outside, but the bedroom curtains were

tightly drawn and a yellow bulb lit the room, giving everything the sepia tone of an old photograph.

I looked for more traces of my old friend. The old Wenzhan was the person I had gone to see. That was whom I wanted to talk to. "Your bedroom's still the same, huh?" I said. "What about that suitcase? You had a thousand years of history written out in there."

"We put my father's old clothes in there. It got burned with him."

"I'm sorry," I said.

I went quiet.

"I thought that was really amazing work," I said.

"Oh, that old crap? I took it all with me to Fuzhou, but I ended up throwing it in the trash."

"That's too bad," I said. I didn't know what else I could say.

We both went quiet for a long time. Perhaps he realized that I had come to him with good intentions, so he tried to come up with a new topic. "I'm working over at the broadcast station," he said. "They read some of your articles on the radio."

"Was that your idea? You know, I'm not exactly a famous author." I thought some self-deprecation might ease the mood.

I started to tell him about my time in Beijing and how hard it had been to make a living.

He was unexpectedly silent. I expected him to say something and for the conversation to get back on track, but the silence only deepened until I felt like it was a yawning chasm that could swallow me whole.

Finally I couldn't stand it any longer. "Well," I said, "sorry for bothering you. I'd better get home."

"Sorry," he said suddenly, "I couldn't explain it even if I wanted to, but I hate you."

I stared back at him, speechless.

"I just want you to tell me," he said, "why it was you and not me."

I knew exactly what he meant. I knew exactly what he wanted me to explain to him. But neither of us had the answer.

The day after I saw Wenzhan, I changed the date of my flight to get back to Beijing a day early. I tried to figure out why I had worried about Wenzhan. Maybe it was because I had always felt guilty for living the life Wenzhan had intended for himself. Maybe it was because both of us were the same in another way: we had both left our hometown looking for a new home, but neither of us had found one.

That was the last time I visited Wenzhan. I would see him when I went back home for the holidays, but I was careful to avoid him. My mother didn't know quite what was happening between us, and she continued bringing me news of Wenzhan and his family. Wenzhan and his brother eventually had a major falling out. His brother had received some money from his wife's family and invested it in a seafood shop. He had done quite well for himself, but perhaps because of their strained relationship when they were younger, he cut Wenzhan out of his life. While his brother was prospering, Wenzhan was struggling, making only about a thousand yuan a month. On top of that, Wenzhan hated his job and looked down on his coworkers. Wenzhan's mother tried to find a woman to marry her son, but his cleft lip and low salary made him an unattractive marriage partner. Eventually, Wenzhan left town again. His destination was not a big city but a small village, where he took a job with the state broadcaster running the local transmitter.

I realized that Wenzhan and I were alike in one way at least: neither of us would ever find a place to truly call home.

# 9

# Hope

I still recall our first meeting and the way he very earnestly introduced himself: "My family name is Zhang. My first name is Hope—yes, just like the English word."

To correctly enunciate his name, he formed his lips into a perfectly round circle.

I figured anyone who went around with a name like that, and who clearly understood its meaning, must be an interesting character. Hope in particular seemed to wear his unusual name like a badge of honor.

He enthusiastically continued his introduction. . . .

He told me his father was a remarkable man who, despite an education limited to elementary school, had taught himself English and, since he was the only person in the village with any proficiency in the language, was given a job teaching at the local school. Apart from teaching English, Hope's father also held the post of school principal. He was a keen reader of contemporary and ancient history and kept himself abreast of current events by listening to the Voice of America. Hope told me that his father was the only man in the village who had any idea how the world worked. There was a tradition in the village of putting up in the yard of each house a sort of mosaic with glazed tiles forming the characters that signified happiness, wealth, and longevity, but Hope's father had done something completely different: he had a local craftsman make him a map of the world.

"The whole world," Hope said, spreading his hands wide, then tracing the shape of the globe. "Every inch." He looked back at me, palms up, as if he had the world balanced in his own two hands. His face glowed with an indescribable light.

I finally realized what he had reminded me of when he had made his introduction: he looked like some government leader addressing a crowd, proudly announcing his name and explaining its meaning.

He had arrived at university with two woven sacks, which he carried into our dormitory, one in each hand. He looked like a Shaolin monk. I could tell his clothes were new and he had gotten a haircut for the big day. The weather had not cooperated. His new clothes had started to stick to him in the heat, and his hair was already in disarray. He must have wanted our first impression of him to be of a handsome, sophisticated young gentleman. He stood in front of me as stiffly as the cowlick in his hair.

His earnest introduction and enthusiastic greeting made me uncomfortable. That is how I always felt around people like him. I couldn't shake the sense that I was the one who was out of line. I liked his smile, though. He had a baby face, but it had been tanned from plenty of time outside, and when he smiled, he showed two deep dimples beside his lips and a pair of tiny white canines. It was a smile that came straight from the heart.

I thought back to my hometown. Economic reforms had transformed it from a poor backwater into a small city of unexpected wealth and prosperity. My own middle school had become the best in town. The rich people did everything they could to get their kids enrolled there.

Those rich kids arrived at school dressed in outfits selected by their parents, their hair done up or slicked down with gel. Some of them even wore bow ties. Their parents wanted them to look like the luckiest kids in the world. The kids walked into school still beaming some residual pride picked up from their parents, but it faded quickly, replaced with nervousness, and then was completely shaken from them by the raucous laughter of their classmates when they caught sight of them. I could always sense the sound of both parents and kids finally breaking.

There is always a standard. If you don't know what the standard is, the harder you try, the more ridiculous you look.

That was how Hope was, too. People like that are always fragile. They are completely pure. They don't know how to judge themselves against the standard.

I'm still not sure when I became so serious and sensible.

On the surface, I seemed casual, even careless. But I

measured each word before speaking to judge whether it would upset anyone. I did my best to say what I thought people wanted to hear. I tried to figure out what was expected of me. I never spoke freely for fear of being disliked by other people. But why did I care whether people liked me? Maybe it was a survival mechanism.

After a while, I felt like I was wearing a mask. Every day when I got home, I would let out a deep sigh. I felt like an actor stepping off stage, safely back behind the curtains. When I went off to middle school and lived for the first time in a communal setting, I couldn't dramatically enter the room and sigh, so I covered it up by sighing discreetly while wiping down my face with a wet cloth. Everyone came to recognize my daily habit of entering our room and wiping my face off. Only one of my classmates ever had the nerve to sneak up beside me and catch me in the act of sighing. He whispered to me, "I heard that. You always cover it up by wiping your face, but I know what it's all about. You can take your mask off." He chuckled and left without saying anything else. I had been discovered.

The classmate who discovered my secret was one of the few students I met in my middle school years who really had something special about him. He had distinguished himself in my eyes during a meeting he had convened at the activity center to celebrate the top students in our grade. When we got there, he ran up to the lectern and said imperiously, as if announcing himself as the second coming of the Buddha, "Upholders of the dharma, I have gathered you here today to share with you that I am the one you have been waiting for. Swear to me you will stay loyal to my one truth path." Some of the students were shocked, but most just rolled their eyes or laughed. Finally some of my classmates started tossing books at him, but he stayed in character, looming over us at the lectern, as still as a statue.

I expected him to grow up to become a cult leader. On the contrary, though, he was the first of my classmates to get married and the first to get fat. He got a job as a biology teacher. He looked forward to the chance to dissect frogs with his class. When we had our ten-year reunion, he had completely lost any traces of specialness. He was drinking and cracking dirty jokes—completely at home in the human world.

I couldn't help but wonder what had happened to him. I had been drinking, so I was bold enough to ask him in a conspiratorial voice, "You were the only one who knew my secret. How'd you turn out like this?"

"I was just joking around," he said, laughing.

He saw the disappointment on my face and became solemn: "Honestly, I couldn't tell you. Maybe I should never have let myself change. But now I don't even know if that was the real me or this is the real me." The way he looked at me gave me goose bumps. He patted me firmly on the shoulder. "What's wrong? You scared? I'm just messing with you."

In fact, I couldn't tell the difference between his truth and his jokes. The chasm between what he had become in reality and my own fantastical expectations of him was simply too vast. But I always believed that people create fantasy worlds for themselves and others. Everyone has a number of fantasy worlds stored in their heads, and I knew he must be the same.

I tried to stay vigilant about the thin barrier between the imaginary and the real. The real world is the only one that can be said to truly exist, but there is always the risk of sinking into untimely fantasy.

On meeting Hope that afternoon, I got a hint as to what kind of fantasies he kept stored in his head. He thought of his arrival at university as his first step into the larger world. He thought he was opening a door to infinite possibilities. He thought when he spoke everyone in the world would hear him.

I couldn't help myself—I had to tell him, "When you introduce yourself to the other students, it might be better if you keep all that stuff about your name to yourself."

"Why?" he said. He turned to face me, and I saw that he was completely baffled by my advice.

"Well, because . . ."

I couldn't bring myself to say it. What I wanted to tell him was, that's not the way the world works.

He went ahead and did it anyway.

When we had our first party, he had a few drinks. Those were probably the first drinks of his life.

When people get a bit of freedom, the first liberty they always exercise is freedom of speech.

His face was flushed red, and he had started to slur his speech. He had launched into his self-introduction again and gotten to the part where his father had a map of the world made. Perhaps it was the liquor, but he was particularly animated. He rose to his feet and spread his arms wide. "It was this big," he said, "the whole world."

Everyone started to laugh.

I don't know if it was because he had been drinking or because he simply lacked any conception of ridicule or mockery, but his classmates' laughter only served to encourage him. He started singing an English song, something like Emilia's "Big Big World," and when it was over, he once again took to his feet, proclaiming his vow to live a beautiful life: "I want to fall in love and lose my virginity as soon as possible. I want to start a band and record an album as soon as possible. I want to publish some poems and put out a collection as soon as possible. I promise that every minute of my life will be magical, and I want to start now."

I suppose the way Hope saw himself, he was a gifted orator channeling Martin Luther King Jr. But I was unimpressed. What a lame imagination, I thought, like something you would find in a middle school textbook.

Gossip about Hope began to circulate through the school. He didn't seem to care. I wondered, did he realize that people were making fun of him, or did he think everyone was amazed by him?

On his way to the school cafeteria, I saw some classmates giggling viciously behind his back. Hope didn't seem to understand their intentions.

Hope rushed over and put his hands on their shoulders and said, "You want to get to know me, brother? Tell me your name. Let's get to know each other." The classmates had no idea how to respond and hurried away. But some people were even more brazen. When they saw Hope coming, they would shout, copying a line from a popular manga, "We must stay hot-blooded!"

Hope responded with dead seriousness, yelling back, "We do it for youth!"

I felt embarrassed on his behalf.

I don't know whether I was worried about Hope or simply curious about how he was going to handle his newfound infamy, but I started hanging out with him.

I was as pragmatic and anxious as ever. I started to calculate how much time in a day I needed to sleep and how much time I could spend studying, balancing that against what kind of grades I could get and what kind of internship I might be able to get myself into. . . . When everything was totaled up, I decided I didn't have enough time. I knew this was a dangerous experiment that would change the course of my life. Since my father had his stroke while I was in high school, most of my savings had been spent, so I knew I had to get a job as soon as I left university. I felt like I was at the controls of a rocket, soaring upward while still trying to make the minute calculations to keep everything on track.

Hope had the opposite approach. It wasn't that he had nothing to worry about; he simply had no idea what he should be worried about. He had no interest in taking a pragmatic approach to planning out his life.

Hope joined the guitar club. It made sense; he wanted to start a band. And he joined the street dance club and the tae kwon do club, too. He even shared with me a fantasy of wearing a tae kwon do outfit during sex. He said it loud, as if he didn't care who could hear. His mind was full of strange fantasies at that time. He thought joining the street dance club or the tae kwon do club represented some kind of cosmopolitan youthful rebellion. He even joined the poetry club.

He dragged me along with him to the club meetings. This was all part of the plan he had proclaimed at the party: to live his life beautifully. I realized after attending a few of the meetings with him that the guitar club might as well be called the "pretending to play guitar club," and the same went for the other clubs. They were meant for people who wanted to hang out with other people interested in pretending to street dance or pretending to do tae kwon do or pretending to write poems.

The entire country at the time was on a track of rapid urbanization, and it seemed as if everyone wanted to get on board with the new cosmopolitanism, even if all they were doing was pretending. Perhaps the best way to describe those clubs he joined where everyone was pretending was collective hypnosis. The club members wanted to join the cult of modernity and worship at the altar of the fashionable.

Being taken prisoner by a fantasy is absurd, especially when it differs so wildly from what is taking place in reality.

I had set a goal for myself of scoring high enough to get a scholarship for both semesters. That was how I paid for my living expenses. I got a job and managed to save about three thousand yuan. My plan was to save up enough to carry myself during an internship at a newspaper. Internships were unpaid, but they were the perfect opportunity to experience something real: real human affairs, real life, the real world. I wanted to bring myself into closer contact with what was real.

Hope and I lived our lives as we thought they should be lived, and we rushed off in opposite directions.

It was no easy feat, but I eventually secured an interview with a company offering internships. Hope came with me to the interview. On the way back to school, I expected him to congratulate me, but instead he shook his head ruefully and said, "My father told me a story once that he heard on Voice of America. There's a guy fresh from an Ivy League school who shows up at a Fortune 500 company hoping to get a job. The CEO asks him, 'So, what did you do in your freshman year?' The guy answers that he buried himself in his books and didn't look up. 'What about your sophomore year?' the CEO asks him. The guy tells the CEO that he started an internship. 'What about your junior year?' the CEO asks. The guy starts telling him about a business plan he wrote up as a way to get ready for the business world after he graduated. And finally the CEO asks him, 'So you're saying you wasted your youth?' The guy shakes his head no. 'Have you sowed your wild oats?' The guy shakes his head no again. The CEO dismisses him, but before leaving he says, 'The problem is you haven't even lived yet, so how do you expect to offer anything to my company? You've got your diploma, but you haven't done a single course in the school of life. Go out there and live, then come back to me.'"

I knew what he was driving at, but honestly, I was skeptical as to how much truth there was to the story of the CEO and the graduate. Hope took it as the gospel truth.

The moral of the story was about discovering how the real world works, but Hope himself had no idea what the real world even was.

I didn't bother poking holes in the story, though. Maybe I was waiting for someone to prove to me that there was another way to live, a way that lay beyond my imagination.

When Hope didn't get any pushback from me, he boldly went on. "I want to start a band," he said. He had all the confidence of youth, and maybe he wanted to show off to me.

A short time after I arrived at university, a Taiwanese café chain opened a site near our school and visited the campus to look for staff. They had three requirements: a dignified bearing, the ability to hold a conversation, and basic stipulations about physical attractiveness, which was referred to euphemistically as "regular physical appearance." The salary was a thousand yuan a month and the shifts were flexible, so students could fit the work into their class schedule. When Hope marched off to the interview, he dragged me along with him. I arrived to see a gaggle of other students also hoping to be hired by the café. Sucking in their guts and talking to each other in syrupy, affected tones, they looked more like they were auditioning for a play than hoping to get a job making coffee.

He barely managed to convince the hiring manager that he met the first two requirements, but when it came to the third, there was no way to bullshit his way through it. I heard the sound of things crashing around inside the café and then Hope screaming, "Fuck that, five foot five!" The hiring manager had produced a tape measure and found Hope lacking. Hope lost his temper and started cursing him out. He emerged from the café laughing and dragged me along behind him saying, "Screw it!"

Hope didn't get the job at the café, but he was suddenly busier than ever. He was usually gone from our shared dorm room by the time I got up, and he didn't get back until after I was asleep. A collection of musical instruments suddenly appeared in our room. When I finally saw him again, I noticed that he had lost weight and his dark tan had deepened. I asked him what he was up to, but the only response he would give was a sly smile. Finally, by chance, on my way to the quarry behind the school to interview someone else, I caught sight of Hope. He was swinging a hammer over his head and bringing it down on a massive rock.

I was shocked. I ran over and said, "You really got yourself into it this time, huh?" He was drenched in sweat and had a towel wrapped around his head like a farmer.

"I don't want to live in their fuckin' world. They think this'll stop me? Those people might be sophisticated, but they're afraid of their own shadow. I can be sophisticated when I want to, but I can get down and dirty when I need to. I can stoop lower than them."

He gave his usual hearty laugh.

When you encounter obstacles and find yourself too weak to overcome them, you risk becoming an object of ridicule; if you can work your way through it, people begin to idolize you. That wasn't how I always thought, but Hope changed my mind.

Hope had begun collecting instruments over the final semester of his first year, and at the start of the second year, he created a poster to recruit band members. He went down to the club recruitment meeting and started yelling about his band.

The poster he had designed was simple. At the top of the page, he wrote, "This is a band that will change the world and transform its members."

Below it, he wrote some song lyrics:

*You ask me, how far do you want to run?*
*I answer you, farther than the eye can see.*
*You ask me, how wide is the world in which you want to live?*
*I answer you, bigger than you could ever imagine.*

He knew how to play a few songs on the guitar, but he wasn't quite sure how to form a band. I knew he had purchased the instruments following an online guide.

The first member of the band was Little Five, a pale, skinny, bespectacled boy whose parents were government employees. He had no real musical background. Hope had spotted him the day before going to the club recruitment meeting while he was staking out a spot. Hope noticed the pale boy changing clothes. Little Five folded the clothes he had changed out of, arranging them as carefully and neatly as if he were handling blocks of tofu. He did a few hops to get warmed up, then ran onto the field. He roared hysterically. When Hope saw Little Five's fierce expression and the veins in his neck sticking out, he knew he had to get him in the band. He rushed over to make his pitch.

The next member recruited was nicknamed Skinny Fat. His father was a national *wushu* coach. He was known for his habit of commenting on the appearance of female classmates. "Her face is good," he might say, "but her nose is too short, so the space between her nose and mouth is too big, and she's got a nice mouth, but the balance is all off. It's too bad, really." Or he would say, "She's got something special, but her legs are too short for her body. You can tell by the way she has the waist of her skirt hiked all the way up. I wouldn't even bother trying to pick her up. . . ."

The third member of the band was nicknamed Oval. His parents ran a convenience store. He ended up writing a bunch of songs about snacks, which he claimed belonged to the genre of lyrical materialism. *"Crunchy shrimp crackers,"* one song went, *"your deep, vast eyes. Crisp, crisp potato chips, crumbling like your words. The vast sky, like peanut shells on the floor around you. The river keeps flowing, and the thick smell of beer rises up. . . ."*

Rounding out the group were Crook, Short Road, and Flat Nose.

Hope had his heart set on being the group's lead singer. That dream was shattered after the band took a trip to a karaoke booth to check their chemistry. As soon as Hope opened his mouth, his bandmates realized that they couldn't entrust vocal duties to him. "You've got the complete package," Skinny Fat said, "completely out of tune and completely unpleasant to listen to." After that, Flat Nose took over as the lead singer. He wasn't much of a singer either, but his particular anatomy gave him an interesting tone.

The band got set up in the dorm room that Hope and I shared. Supposedly, they met every day at four in the afternoon and banged away until nine at night. I heard they were always battling neighboring rooms' noise complaints, though, so the practice time was usually limited to a few hours at most. Sometimes they would even march down the hallway to get in fights with their classmates.

I have to say "supposedly" and "I heard" because I was never around for their practices. My internship at the newspaper had turned into a part-time job. Every afternoon when I didn't have class, I ran around the city looking for stories: retired cadres who cultivated rare orchids, an old man whose granddaughter had fallen in love with an old friend as ancient as him, an important speech by a local politician, a street fight that resulted in casualties, and plenty of traffic accidents.

A female reporter on the staff took me under her wing, but whenever we reported from the scene of a traffic accident, she simply couldn't handle it, especially if there were casualties. The volume of her screams was inversely proportional to her distance from the body. I was calmer than I ever could have imagined. I took everything in and jotted down notes. I didn't mind using my pen to lift the blanket covering a body, either. I was able to keep my cool because I never took the body as a real person; it was simply another item at the accident scene. I was fine at the scene of car crashes, but when I got back to school and saw my classmates rushing around in a fog of hormones, it was harder to stay calm. I thought to myself sometimes, *These people are wasting the best years of their lives. What's the point?*

In that state of mind, I couldn't help but find myself admiring Hope's strange ambitions.

I was worried about him. I was both envious and skeptical, but deep down, I wanted to see how his life would play out. What was he truly capable of?

Watching him felt like watching God forming one of his creations. But when the realization slipped in that he was actually my friend, I had an overwhelming feeling of anxiety on his behalf.

Three months after they started practicing in our dorm, they put on their first concert. I figured that despite all the noise complaints, they must have worked hard in the time they had. I made sure I was there to see their first performance. I was going to sit front row, dead center, and was even given a special duty: Hope gave me a bouquet of flowers, and I was supposed to get onstage at the climax of the show to present it to the band. I wasn't particularly enthusiastic. I was worried about what people would think of me. Hope insisted, though. "You will sit in the audience, and then, when your soul explodes with our life force, you race to the stage and give us our flowers."

The venue for the concert was one of the school's cafeterias. The stage was simply the space that was usually reserved for students to line up to swipe their meal plan cards. They used a PA system borrowed from the Student Recreation Committee, and the cafeteria tables provided seating. To add some atmosphere, the corridor between the main door and the serving window was hung with posters emblazoned with poetic slogans: "Can you hear the song your spirit sings?" "Squeeze every ounce out of youth, let your ignorance drain from your soul," "Loneliness is the truth that all hearts carry." It looked to me like something from a pyramid scheme.

It was at the concert that I first heard the name Hope had chosen for the band: the World. It reminded me of Hope gesticulating wildly as he described his father's map of the world.

Despite being passed over for lead singer, Hope still had much to say, so he played the role of host for the concert.

The instruments were arranged, colored lights lit the room, and Hope led the band members to the makeshift stage. He took the microphone and put everything into a full-throated roar: "Hello everyone! We are the World. Listen to our song!"

Thinking back, I can't recall the details of any of the songs they played, but everything was a cover of an old pop song with new lyrics by Hope. Hope wasn't a skilled lyricist, but he had a talent for laying bare his soul. However, those over-the-top lyrics weren't a good fit with the simple backing music. All I remember of the concert was Hope's opening roar: "We are the World. Listen to our song!"

I might not have been able to admit it at the time, but the way Hope took the stage and addressed the audience stirred something in me. It made me think. Could I strip myself of all the limitations I had placed on myself? Could I free myself of all my inhibitions?

I wasn't alone. The songs weren't memorable, and the band never really amounted to much, but Hope became something of a campus legend.

The day after the concert, people started waving to him on the way to class or calling out greetings. Word of the band even spread to the highest levels of the school: at a meeting of the Chinese Department discussing how to deal with SARS, the department head worked them into his opening remarks. "I've heard our Chinese Department has made contact with the World," he said, "or perhaps it's the other way around. I'm talking about the band, of course."

There was never even a hint of modesty or embarrassment when Hope received positive attention or affirmation. He didn't strike a pretentious pose either. He simply smiled, showing off his little fangs, and said, "Yep, that was me. I'm Hope. I'm the World."

This is the way I saw it: Hope had turned his life over to chasing a dream, and whether or not he succeeded, the purity of his emotions made the feeling contagious. People believed in him, and he became the spokesperson for them and for the fantasy world he was trying to communicate to them.

That was what I liked about Hope. I believed in him, but at the same time, I was worried that he was burning too bright, giving himself over to lighting the path for others. If he failed, the people who followed him would be disappointed—but how would Hope feel?

Hope fell in love, just as he had planned.

After he became a campus celebrity, our dorm room became a sort of student salon, the destination for all the notable characters at our school. As many people as were coming and going from the dorm, one of them was bound to catch Hope's eye. After that, it wasn't long until he hooked up with them.

While Hope was falling in love, I found myself spending

less and less time at our dorm. A story I had written for the newspaper had won a provincial journalism award, and my editor had given me even more assignments. I usually didn't get back to the dorm until ten or so at night, but I always found the party still going when I arrived and always peopled by a new group of visitors.

It was a varied crowd: chatty classmates who wanted to pepper Hope with questions about the meaning of life; people with piercings and sleeves of tattoos who aspired to drag Hope into some badass enterprise with them; nerdy students that everyone avoided for fear of being dragged into a dull conversation, who timidly asked if Hope was interested in taking part in their experiments; and a number of hangers-on who wanted to talk Hope into some music industry project. . . . They all had their own private dreams and fantasies, but they were never prepared to carry them out. They were "still laying the groundwork" for such and such a project or "just waiting for the right time" to pursue whatever dream. Their pitch to Hope was always the same: "You should do it first!"

They circled around Hope, as if waiting for him to save them. They reached out to him, trying to get him interested in their own schemes and dreams. The school's rule was lights out at ten, but that didn't put an end to the gatherings. The darkness seemed to encourage people to open up even more. It was when the lights went out that everyone seemed to abandon rational thought and give in to fantasy. I was often startled awake by someone shouting something like "We owe it to ourselves to achieve our dreams" or "You're only young once!"

Hope would answer them with even more enthusiasm, saying, "You're absolutely right!"

I was burning the candle at both ends, trying to keep up with my schoolwork and the job at the newspaper. I was getting sick of the passionate nightly colloquies. When final exams approached in my second year, I decided it was time to rent a room off campus.

Hope felt like I was abandoning him. On the day I moved out, he cautiously asked me, "You don't believe in me anymore or what? Is it just too noisy for you?"

Hope could accept the latter but not the former.

I did my best to explain the situation—all the extra work at the newspaper and how important it was for me to get a good night's sleep—but he still seemed to be seeking my approval. Perhaps he wasn't sure exactly how to get it, since he just asked me again, "You still believe in me, right?"

"Of course," I said.

"So you've still got my back, right?"

I knew I could end up going back and forth with him all day, but I suddenly came up with a way to cut the conversation short and maybe even earn a byline. I could imagine the headline: "The Passionate Youth Behind the Campus Band." I decided an interview with him would provide some nice background for the story. I asked Hope if he was up for it. "I want other people to hear your story," I told him.

At first he seemed stunned, but then he smiled, show-ing his canines. "Really?" he asked. "I'd love that."

After that, my transition out of the dorm was smooth. When I left, Hope took brush and ink and produced a poster to hang on the door. It read, "Spirit Quest Pavilion."

The next time I heard from him was three days after moving out. My phone rang at two in the morning.

"What are you doing?" he asked.

I knew there was something on his mind. "What is it?" I asked.

"I just did it. . . ."

I knew he wanted to tell me that he had gotten laid, but I wanted to get off the phone. "Good night," I said.

"Don't hang up," he yelped anxiously. As I reached for the button, I heard him screaming on the other end of the line: "This is what it means to be young! I'm doing some-thing meaningful."

I only spent as much time on campus as I absolutely had to, but even still, I heard highly exaggerated accounts of Hope's exploits: he had run through three girls in one week, he got in a brawl at a restaurant, he took over the lectern in a literature class to sing one of his own compositions. . . . There was also an incident in which he kissed a male class-mate. A group of people was watching. He responded as he usually did: "I want to experience everything life has to offer."

The school counselor finally couldn't take it any longer. He decided to call Hope's family. The phone rang way off in his mountain village, and Hope's father picked it up. When the school counselor briefed the rural English instructor on the conduct of his son, Hope's father started to laugh.

I figured it must be a case of Hope's father hoping to live vicariously through his son. His dreams had never been realized, but perhaps in his son they would be.

The counselor eventually tracked me down, hoping I could offer Hope some advice. He knew I tended to be more forward thinking than Hope. "We've all been young, of course," the counselor said, "but there are limits. You've got a good head on your shoulders. You know what it'll mean for him to have those sorts of things on his public record. It could have a negative impact on his future. He's disconnected from reality. He has to know reality will catch up with him in the end." I knew the counselor had Hope's best interests in mind, but I also knew my words would fall on deaf ears. The only reason Hope and I had ever been friends was because we were complete opposites.

Hope once again surprised us all.

He abruptly calmed down and turned down the volume on his life. Nobody could have expected that a girl had flipped the switch. Her name was Wang Ziyi.

Like Hope, Wang Ziyi was something of a campus celebrity. The reason for her notoriety was not any innate charm or great beauty. She was famous because of her father. Rumor had it that he was secretary-general of the city's Municipal Party Committee. This was never actually confirmed, but even professors deferred to her.

For all Wang Ziyi's notoriety on campus, nobody seemed to know her well. She was often referred to as simply "the daughter of the secretary-general." She seemed to hold herself above her fellow students, and she often tilted her head in a way that made it appear as if she was purposely avoiding meeting anyone's gaze. Hope and Wang Ziyi seemed to be products of two different worlds. Where Wang Ziyi came from, people of her generation were waiting to inherit power, either directly from their parents or from the families they had married into. To her classmates, there was something old fashioned about people like Wang Ziyi, but that didn't stop them from envying her identity.

Despite all that, Wang Ziyi became Hope's girlfriend.

At first the romance surprised me, but I eventually came to realize something about Hope. Some people make a breakthrough into a so-called new world, but they always end up looking back, and when they do, they realize that they are still judging their new reality by the rules they used to live by. Even if you fight your way into a new reality, you are always bound by the rules of the old. Nobody understood that about Hope. He couldn't lead them into a new reality because he was still tethered to the old reality. I suppose even Hope might not have realized it.

There was an easy explanation for Hope and Wang Ziyi getting together. Hope thought he could use her to prove that he had given up his old reality, and Wang Ziyi was with him as an act of rebellion against the reality she lived in. Wang Ziyi was even more of a rebel than Hope was, in fact—but maybe most of the people that visited the Spirit Quest Pavilion were more rebellious than Hope, or they understood what freedom really meant.

The love affair exposed another side of Hope to his classmates. The flow of visitors to his dorm slowed to a trickle. Those who stayed away might have whispered things about staying away because of a fear that the crude decadence which had infected Hope—passed on from Wang Ziyi and her old-fashioned world—might be contagious. But perhaps deep down they realized it was Hope that was the source, not Wang Ziyi.

Around the time Hope and Wang Ziyi got together, I realized that I had my own admirer. Her name was Zhang Jingyi. She came from the same world as Wang Ziyi: her father was the director of the Municipal Bureau of Culture. She collected clippings of the poems and short stories I had published in the newspaper's literary supplement.

I had only just settled into my rented room when she showed up uninvited. She didn't say much, but I noticed her eyes darting around, scanning the small space. She didn't stay long but then returned that afternoon with a quilt, a mosquito net, a pillow, an incense burner, and a fountain pen. I didn't know what to say. It was too late to refuse, though, and I could only watch in silence as she began putting each item away. She seemed to know exactly where each thing belonged.

She sat down and began talking. She told me her father always advised her to find a partner with talent. Her father's rationale was that a potential husband's background was secondary to his potential. "He told me that was the best way to start a family with a future," she said. "Being able to pick a man like that is an important ability for a woman."

I realized what kind of person I was dealing with. Even though I had always been pragmatic and calculating, constantly concerned about my future, I somehow still resented that side of me. If I had been as coldly calculating as I sometimes aspired to be, I would have snatched up Zhang Jingyi in an instant. She was a good girl, not spoiled, modest, traditional, and focused on building a family. But hearing those words come out of her mouth, it all sounded so foreign to me. I awkwardly showed her the door.

After Jingyi left, I had the urge to call Hope and invite him out for drinks. Our two relationships provided an interesting contrast, but both of us had a fundamental misunderstanding of ourselves. He thought he was breaking all the rules while living according to every single one; I thought I was making my way forward with the utmost care, when all I really wanted was to break every single convention.

In the end, I decided not to call him. I wasn't really sure why. Maybe nobody really knows why they do the things they do. I wasn't sure what I was doing: Was it better to simply live happily or to keep pushing myself even if it meant that I had to grind unhappily through the rest of my life?

Meanwhile, Hope's reputation at school had gone into free fall. I never would have predicted how precipitous his decline would be. By the start of our third year, Hope was no longer a campus celebrity. Those who had once gathered for the late-night sessions at our dormitory began to resent him. They muttered in private that he hadn't amounted to much and tried to figure out why they had ever worshipped him. One of them even said, "He was our hero back then. I think it must have been that concert, but the songs weren't even very good. They couldn't even sing. Why did we ever fall for it?"

Wang Ziyi, more than even Hope himself, seemed unwilling to let things end so ignominiously. She pushed Hope to get the band together and practice even harder. She finagled some money from her father to invest in more professional instruments for them. The World reunited for a concert shortly before midterm exams.

The reunion was far more professional than the last performance. Rather than the cafeteria, they were set to play in the school auditorium. Wang Ziyi had secured the auditorium, and her reputation and guidance helped launch a comprehensive advertising campaign. The school's TV and radio stations both talked nonstop about the upcoming concert. There were posters for the show on every bulletin board on campus, and members of the student union had been dispatched to put them up in nearby businesses.

The poster featured a picture of the band with Hope in

the center and the other members arrayed on either side. "The World" was written in massive text across the top, and below it, "We live according to our ambitions. This is youth." In the picture Hope was smiling, showing his canines, but perhaps because of the makeup he was wearing, his face seemed slightly blurry.

I ended up missing the concert. I had to work overtime at the newspaper. According to our classmates, the show was a disaster. The auditorium had a capacity of a thousand, but it wasn't even half full, and many of those filling out the audience had been pressed to come by members of the student union.

The next day at school, I noticed that someone had drawn a big X over one of the posters. Below the X was written, "Funded by bureaucrats—who are you fooling?"

What Wang Ziyi didn't understand was that a band like the World didn't need professionalism. They weren't selling music; they were selling a feeling of freedom. Maybe Hope didn't realize it, either.

The only thing I could do for him was to live up to the commitment I had made on the day I left the dorm. Shortly after the concert, my newspaper published a long article on the World. I had pushed a more veteran reporter to interview Hope. I didn't think I was up to the task. I wasn't ready to ask Hope any hard questions.

In the interview quoted in the article, the reporter asked Hope how he chose the band's name. Hope answered, "The World—well, the world is something that's so big and complicated that it's always beyond your wildest imagination. It's chaotic and limitless."

When the paper hit the newsstands, Hope regained some measure of celebrity. Wang Ziyi seemed to count it as a victory. She was seen in the days that followed conspicuously hanging out with Hope.

Shortly after that, I began to hear rumors that Hope and Wang Ziyi might be having problems. Wang Ziyi's father was not impressed with his daughter's recent behavior and went to the school to complain that Hope had led his daughter astray. The school had been started as an academy for training future teachers and still produced a number of graduates who went into teaching. It had always been a fairly conservative institution, so there already was an item in the rule book about "inappropriate courtship behavior." On top of that, the school didn't want to risk offending a member of the municipal bureaucracy. The school came down hard on Hope, ending his scholarship and preventing him from joining the party.

Wang Ziyi had lost patience with her boyfriend, too, it seemed, and she started to nitpick and nag at Hope. She started many sentences with "You should have . . ." For example, "You should have realized how this school is run. What are you so worried about, anyway?" Or "You should be immune to this kind of thing by now. It's not like you're going to starve to death because you lost a scholarship."

I couldn't do much to help him. I had planned to spend most of the final year of university doing an internship.

Most of the internships lasted three or four months, then you might be offered a permanent job. But there was only so much time in the year, so I knew I only had three shots at landing a job. I also knew I'd have to watch my bank account to make sure I had enough to support myself while doing the unpaid internship.

I wanted to have enough time in my final year to focus on my internship, so I started writing my undergraduate dissertation in my junior year. The effort to get ahead on my work occupied most of my free time, but I occasionally went with Jingyi to get something to eat or go for a walk.

In the second semester of that year, Jingyi invited me to a concert. A pianist from Germany was putting on a recital. It had become a major event in the city. I agreed to accompany her, but Jingyi suggested we meet up beforehand to take a stroll. I wasn't sure what she had in mind. When I asked, she told me, "I want to take you shopping for something to wear to the concert. Some of my older relatives are going to be at the concert. . . ."

I knew immediately the purpose of the concert date.

I thought very calmly and rationally about my future with Jingyi. I felt guilty about not evaluating her on her own merits but by the role she would play in the plan I had laid out for my life.

I agreed to go shopping with her, and I let her choose something appropriate to wear to the concert, but I insisted on paying for it. I knew that letting her pay would be crossing a symbolic line in our relationship.

I'll never forget how Jingyi looked on the night of the concert. She was beautiful—stunning even—in a simple white gown and elegant black heels, with a blossom pinned at her temple. She was the picture of grace as she met me at the main doors to the theater. She played her role perfectly, keeping me by her side but never closer than would be appropriate for our relationship and the occasion. She introduced me to each of her relatives: there was a deputy commissioner at the Provincial Bureau of Public Works, the dean of an art school, the head of a government department in Beijing. . . . Everyone greeted me with soft-spoken politeness and the slightest gentle verbal push in the direction of Jingyi. Her family had an easygoing but sophisticated way about them.

When the performance ended, Jingyi walked me out. "Everyone was quite fond of you," she said. "My uncle told me he could get you an internship with the Bureau of Public Works. He said he should be able to arrange a few more, too." She blushed.

I thought I would be able to play it off with more ease. "It's too early for me to make a decision," I said abruptly, then wished her a good night.

On my way to catch the bus home from the theater, I was racked by anxiety. I walked toward the bus stop at the intersection pondering my future. I looked up to see someone ahead of me in a tuxedo and dress shoes but crying like a child. I realized it was Hope.

I caught up with him and said, "What's wrong, Hope?"

He turned to look at me and started wailing, looking

even more like a little boy. Just like me, Hope had been brought to the concert by a girl. Wang Ziyi had instructed Hope before they arrived on how to act to impress her father, who would also be in attendance. He waited in front of the theater, and when she arrived, she immediately said, "You look ridiculous in that suit. What did I ever see in you? Why did I even bother? Do you know what I put my father through, just because I wanted to be with you?" Wang Ziyi told Hope to leave. He realized that it was the end of their relationship.

I didn't bother trying to comfort Hope. I saw the breakup as an inevitability. Wang Ziyi had already realized that her relationship with Hope did not, in fact, represent a revolt against her upbringing, and he was far from the free agent she had imagined him to be. Wang Ziyi was still in search of her rebellion.

When I went home over the break, I told my parents about Jingyi. They were excited, especially when they saw her picture.

I was still hesitant to commit, though.

I shut myself up in my room at home and pondered the choices I had to make. I knew the decisions I made during that time would determine what I became. I knew my choice of Jingyi would be a choice for life.

Two days before the semester was to begin and I was due back at school, I went to the bank and transferred my savings into a single account. Subtracting enough to pay the final year's tuition, I had twelve thousand yuan left.

I figured that was enough for me to gamble. Deep down, I knew what I was thinking. . . .

I packed my bag and went back to school a day early. When I got there, I set up a date with Jingyi. I hadn't come to a final decision yet, and I wanted to wait until I saw her.

Jingyi really was an intelligent young woman. She seemed to realize why I had called her. She had carefully arranged even this date. She told me to bring my bike over so we could ride out to the seaside park together and go for a stroll. She even brought some of my poems with her so she could read them while looking out on the ocean.

It was a beautiful day. There was a pleasant view. There was a pleasant breeze. She wanted everything to be perfect. She stopped and turned to me and asked, "So what did you want to tell me?"

I looked back at her, feeling a rising wave of disgust and guilt. All of that disgust and guilt was directed at myself. I hated myself for being so cold and calculating—and even still, I couldn't manage to follow through on the plans I had made for myself. I knew that I was about to hurt an innocent girl.

Finally I couldn't delay any longer.

I was impressed by her poise and intelligence again. She never stopped smiling. She turned her back on me, walked to her bike, and rode away. We never spoke again. Two weeks after that, when I had settled everything on campus, I went and bought a train ticket to Beijing.

The long period of apathy and fatigue that followed my breakup with Jingyi was, I later realized, what romance novels might call heartbreak. I never expected it to happen to me.

The day before I left for Beijing, I packed up all the stuff in my rented room and dropped it off at the dorm room I once shared with Hope. I wanted to say goodbye to him, and I wanted to know what had become of him.

Hope smiled, showing his canines. He had undertaken an unauthorized renovation of the dorm, taking apart my bed so he'd have more room to store instruments. As soon as I walked in, he wanted to play drums for me, then he told me he had a new song to show me on guitar.

It wasn't long before he set down his guitar and sat down on the drum kit stool. He was trying to put on a brave face, but I could see depression creeping in.

He told me the band had broken up. He filled me in on what the former members were up to: one had gotten an internship through his parents' connections, another was getting ready to do a master's, then maybe get a job as a civil servant. . . . Being in the band had been a youthful indulgence for them, and they eventually cast it aside. They saw the future looming, and they took off on their own trajectories. They were consumed by something else: pursuing what it was they wanted out of life.

Hope became like the last person left at a party, cleaning up the mess.

"So, what've you got planned?" I asked him.

He glared at me for a moment, not speaking, then tried to affect a breezy air and told me, "I'll look for new members. I'm going to keep playing. Don't forget whom you're talking to—I'm Hope!"

I could tell that he didn't really mean it. He wasn't fooling anyone, least of all me. I could see that his old resolve was gone.

I struggled for a while to come up with a response. Perhaps the thing to say at that moment would have been "You should be practical. You have your future to think about." But I spared him. I said goodbye and left.

Why did I feel as if I had to go to Beijing? I wasn't even sure myself. I thought it was the best place to make a complete break.

After I arrived, I realized that my judgment had been correct. Beijing is a place where everything is taken to its conclusion. I was forced to meet challenges head-on and try to translate my dreams into direct action. In Beijing, everything is done at a national level. When people in Beijing talk about changing the world, they really mean it. They don't simply scatter their words to the wind. They act.

Beijing caused an almost hormonal response in me. I had the sense that the world truly was infinite—it felt like vertigo. In a city like Beijing, I had to be brave.

My chance to live in—or be swallowed by—Beijing came in the form of an offer to intern for a magazine.

At first, I felt like everyone in the city was like an ant: a head swollen with dreams being dragged along on a skinny body that was rushing every which way. I became one of those ants.

After I arrived in Beijing, I thought about Hope every now and then. I wasn't sure whether it would be a good idea to encourage him to come to a place like Beijing. Superficially, Beijing was fueled by dreams, so it would seem to be a natural fit for someone like Hope, but I knew the way those dreams became reality in a place like Beijing was through fierce determination. You had to take that determination and rush forward, even if it entailed great sacrifice. I was worried that Hope, who spent most of his time in a fantasy world, wouldn't be ready for the tedious requirements of turning his dreams into reality. I wondered if he would ever have the patience to really work for what he dreamed of, if he would be able to accept the sacrifices. It's not enough to have a dream; you need persistence.

The December after I arrived in Beijing, I talked to Hope on the phone. He was still talking about recruiting new members for the band. "People need to hear our song," he said, brimming with optimism. He changed the topic after that and asked me what my life in Beijing was like. "I've been trying to imagine," he said, "what it's like there."

"Well," I told him, "I don't know what to tell you. . . . It's just a lot of hard work, always trying to get to the next rung on the ladder, but it's different here, because even if you're only taking little steps forward, it feels like you're working toward a clear goal."

"You ever get the feeling like you've got the whole world in the palm of your hand?"

I didn't know quite how to answer him. I knew anybody who would ask a question like that had absolutely no idea what was required to turn dreams into reality.

I knew what my answer to the question should be, but I refused to actually say it. "Hope, you could be here, too. All those dreams you have, you can accomplish them, too, but it takes more than simply having them or even throwing yourself into something. You have to be pragmatic. You have to be willing to lower yourself to another level sometimes, so that you feel so pathetic you can barely stand yourself."

I finally decided to invite him to Beijing. I was worried that Hope had grown too big for a small city but might one day find it impossible to leave.

"Why don't you come to Beijing? I'm renting a place here, and you can crash with me for a while."

Without even pausing to consider, he said, "Sure!"

I started planning for his stay long before he arrived, as was my habit. When I got off work, I began preparing my rented apartment. I wanted both of us to have our own space. I went to a furniture store and got a mattress, then went to a secondhand store to pick up a bookshelf. I packed the bookshelf with books and put it between the two mattresses as a makeshift divider. I moved the apartment's low dinner table into my space; I put a chair on his side, thinking he could use it if he wanted to play guitar.

But Hope never arrived. I called him, but he didn't answer.

I eventually had to ask some other classmates what was going on with Hope. In the time since I had last spoken to him, his life had gone off the rails. He got into another brawl off campus, he had dated another string of women, and his professors were all sick of him. He was running headfirst down a slippery slope. He wanted to feel alive again. He regained his status as a campus celebrity at least. But his glory proved to be short-lived: he was suspended from school a few months before he was set to graduate.

I received that final detail from Wang Ziyi. Her real intention in texting me had been to ask about Beijing. She wanted to come to Beijing, too. I figured she wanted to get into a language school in preparation for going overseas, or maybe she still had some urge to rebel and wanted to go to Beijing to fool around. "My parents can decide for themselves what they want to do," she told me in the text.

The news about Hope came like a casual postscript at the very end of the text: "Hope got suspended. Did you ever think that'd happen? He actually sneaked over here to see me. He wanted me to ask my father to talk to the school administrators. I know some people think he's just so committed to his own values, but that's not it at all. . . . He's trying to fool himself into believing in himself, as much as he is trying to fool other people. What a hypocrite!"

I tapped into my phone, "He's not pretending. He doesn't know how to deal with all his dreams, his urges. . . . He hasn't figured out how to live in the real world yet. It's normal to have a bunch of conflicting ideas that you can't quite integrate into a complete worldview. He's a bit too naive. He doesn't know who he is yet." I deleted the message without sending it. I didn't owe her an explanation. Wang Ziyi didn't know who she was yet either.

My internship in Beijing was going smoothly, and I decided to volunteer to work over the holiday instead of going back home over the New Year break. I knew it would look good to the higher-ups, and staying in Beijing would let me save what I would have spent on travel expenses.

One night I got a call from my mother grousing about being home alone during the holiday. When I put down the phone, I realized that one year had officially rolled over into the next.

A bowl of instant noodles with two eggs cracked over them was going to be my New Year meal.

My phone suddenly rang again.

It was Hope.

The first thing he said was "Sorry I never called you back last time."

"Why didn't you come to Beijing?" I asked.

"I was broke. You know, I'm not a saver like you are. I've never been that careful."

He went on to vividly narrate his saga of suspension, closing with a scene of the entire school gathered to see him off. "So I was dragging my suitcase behind me," he said, "headed out to the front gate, and when I got out—can you picture this?—I sat myself down, right there, took out my guitar, and put on a concert. When I was done, everyone broke out cheering for me. It's too bad you missed it."

After that, he seemed suddenly exhausted. He sighed. "There's something I want to tell you, but I need you to keep it to yourself."

"What is it?" I asked.

"I think I'm sick. I keep hearing this sound in my head. It sounds like something's crashing around in there."

"How long has it been there? Is it from playing drums?"

"That's not it. It started after I left school. I don't drum anymore. I tried to get a job at a bar, but you know I can't sing. I'm just doing my best to get enough to eat."

I realized what was going on with Hope: his expulsion from university had been a major setback, and he was sinking further and further into his fantasy world and losing contact with reality.

"Shake yourself out of it," I said. "Maybe I can talk to the school for you. If you get back in, you can finish out the year and start saving up money. You can come to Beijing, too." I was trying to put him back on the straight and narrow.

He suddenly lost his temper. "Oh, is that what you think I should do? You want me down in the quarry again swinging that hammer? I can't do it. They want to beat me because I have more freedom than they'll ever have and they can't handle it. We're friends, aren't we? You're acting like you don't understand me at all. I need some money from you. I want to go to Beijing. I need to see a doctor."

I tried to empathize with him. "Hope," I said, "I'm telling you this because you *are* my friend. I can give you the money to come to Beijing, but the problem is—"

He hung up on me.

His phone was powered off when I called back.

I was angry, of course, but I was also confused. I didn't understand why I could never get Hope to see the reality of his situation.

I tried to imagine how he might be living. He had always wanted to charge forward, never willing to settle for a mediocre life. But what he never realized was that achieving dreams required lots of small, mediocre, uninteresting steps.

Hope had the creeping suspicion that he had been branded a loser. At a certain point, he was no longer able to find refuge in fantasy. He became even more anxious and sensitive. He pushed back against any questioning of that fantasy.

Maybe Hope refused to take my call because he had decided that if he was branded a loser, I must be a winner.

Other classmates weren't sure exactly what was going on with Hope, but they occasionally passed on what little they knew. I heard that he sometimes sneaked back onto campus and started trouble, accusing his former classmates of mediocrity and messing with the younger female students. He even invited some of his former classmates out for drinks, but after that he disappeared again. He was spotted at one of the bars in town once, and another time busking on the street with his guitar.

When I still couldn't get in touch with him, I got a number for Hope's father from the school counselor. I wanted to convince Hope's father to talk to his son and try to get through to him exactly how the world worked. When I got through to the rural English instructor Hope had told me so much about, I found it tough to understand him through his thick accent. He sounded like a foreigner speaking Chinese. "Don't worry about it," he told me. "It's just letting off steam. Even if he ends up failing, he has to get it out of his system or he'll wind up thinking he's wasted his life."

Talking to his father, I realized what was at the root of Hope's anxiety and desperation, and why he wanted to embrace fantasy instead of reality. I was sure that his father wouldn't be much help to him.

I wasn't sure what to do, so I decided to call Wang Ziyi for help. "Oh yeah," she said casually, "he showed up here a few times. He stood outside my window playing his guitar, trying to tell me he still loved me. He was drunk and wouldn't leave, so my father called the police, and they dragged him off. He's really an absolute—"

I knew what she was about to say, but I hung up before I heard it.

I was still worried about Hope, but my concern was quickly overwhelmed by my own daily life.

The internship in Beijing was a success, and even before I graduated, they offered me a permanent position. I had to go back to school for the graduation ceremony, and I thought I might be able to see Hope.

I went back to the dorm we had once shared and found it immaculately clean. I heard from someone else that Hope had carefully tidied the room before leaving, scrubbing every inch of it. Nobody understood why he had done it. I didn't get it either.

Hope had taken his guitar with him, but he had unexpectedly left behind all the instruments he had collected since forming the band. He said he hoped someone else might use them, maybe someone who had the same dream as him.

I could imagine something of the conflicted emotions Hope must have felt after being forced to leave school.

When I lived there, I had always felt like my university town was particularly tiny—only one main street with smaller streets coming off it, each one devoted to its own particular purpose—but it felt massive when I was running all over it looking for Hope.

There were only a few bars to check, then the two or

three music shops on Jiuyi Road. Hope didn't have many places to hide, but I still couldn't find him before I had to go back to Beijing.

The show must go on. The intermission ends, and the actor walks back onstage. I had to keep playing my role.

I said goodbye to my school, said goodbye to the city, and said goodbye to Hope.

Beijing truly was a massive beast. The instant the plane touched down in the city, it began to wrap innumerable tentacles around me, dragging me into all sorts of things—new challenges, fresh stories, happiness, sorrow. . . . I sank into the layers of happiness and grief. Beijing wrapped me up inside itself. That's the way Beijing is: you can forget that the outside world still exists.

Many of my former classmates had been training to be teachers, and most had gone on to take jobs in their hometowns, but a few of them wound up temporarily in Beijing, sometimes to continue their studies, sometimes for a course. I was the only one to take root in the capital. I served as an informal welcoming committee for former classmates passing through Beijing.

I didn't go out of my way to ask them about Hope, but they occasionally brought him up. I wasn't that close to most of those classmates, so old times and people we both knew were about all we had to talk about.

I heard from them that Hope had continued drifting through life. When he finally had nowhere else to stay, Hope called his father from a pay phone and asked him to take him back.

Hope's mother and father had a vicious argument about what to do with their son. His mother finally prevailed, though, and called in some favors to get Hope a job teaching at a small school in a village outside Sanming. His lessons ranged from language and politics to music.

I was so busy with my own life that my head felt ready to burst, but I sometimes thought of Hope. I would suddenly imagine him in the village school, leading some kids in a song. In my imagination, he had never lost his passion. He was smiling, showing his canines, his face lit up. I smiled, too, when I imagined the scene.

I felt like I could feel what he must have felt in that moment.

I put my head down and got through the next two years in Beijing. One otherwise normal night, my phone rang. The head of the student association at my university was on the line. "Any chance you can come back here this weekend? I want to take you to Sanming."

I didn't realize at first what he meant. "What's going on?" I asked.

"Hope's dead. The alumni association is planning to take a trip over there to look in on his family. Since you two were such good friends, I thought you might want the chance to see him off."

I felt as if I had been hit on the head with a hammer. My mind went blank.

The student association head filled me in on what Hope had been up to. It was not at all what I had imagined. Hope had gone to the village and became uncharacteristically taciturn, which was not a particularly big problem, but when he did start talking, it was to tell his family about the sound in his head—like a crashing, he said, as if there were a beast locked up inside his skull. He started to get headaches late at night that accompanied the crashing sounds, and then the episodes started to happen during the daytime. He would smash his head against the wall until he was bleeding.

By the end, Hope was unable to continue teaching. His father took him to a clinic, but the doctor was hesitant to make a diagnosis.

A week before Hope killed himself, he made a final request of his father: "Can you take me to Beijing to see a doctor?"

His father refused.

The family had spent most of their savings looking after Hope. Hope's father had lost all patience with his son.

The association head sighed and said, "We have to look after each other. Life is a long battle. He's the first one of us to fall."


His voice seemed to fade away on the other end of the phone until I could barely make out what he was saying.

Nobody else understood—not his classmates, not Wang

Ziyi, not his own father—but I did: the monster that was crashing around in his head was a product of the fantasy world he had sunk into. He had been feeding it with phantoms all those years, until it had grown too big for his head to contain. He had asked to be taken to Beijing, and I realized it had been his final solution.

An indescribable sadness welled up in my chest. I gaped like a fish, trying to speak, but nothing would come out. I realized in that moment that after all those years of holding things in, I couldn't bring myself to release my emotions. Even in that moment of intense grief, I was still worried about upsetting my neighbors.

During four years of university and two years working in Beijing, I had always kept myself under strict control. I didn't smoke and I didn't drink, and I had never found any way to vent the emotions that had built up. I kept it all inside because I wanted to maintain control. I wanted to keep moving forward toward my final destination.

But what was that destination really? Did any of this have any meaning at all?

I couldn't answer those questions.

I still wasn't willing to cry. I paced back and forth in my hundred-square-foot room. I sighed, deep and long, and it felt like I was finally releasing some of what had built up inside me during those years. The sighs made me feel as if I were venting some noxious steam that had filled my chest cavity. All of the things I had pushed down over the years had congealed inside of me, slowly forming into a marsh so dark and deep that it could swallow the whole world.

I realized that, like Hope, maybe Beijing had been my final solution, too.

Maybe Hope and I had the same sickness.

# 10

# You Can't Hide the Ocean

I grew up on the coast, and my father once made a living as a sailor, but I didn't see the ocean until I was six years old.

The first time I saw the ocean was on the way to see my grandmother. My mother and I were walking down a path between the villages that was separated from the sea by a thicket of sugarcane. I did not know the ocean was so close, but I knew something was shimmering through the sugarcane. I waited until my mother was distracted, then charged through to take a look.

My mother huffed and puffed after me, trying to chase me down before I made it there. When she caught up with me, she explained that it had been my father's decision to hide the ocean from me. He was afraid, my mother said, that I would run into the water, and there was a chance something could happen to me. It was more complicated than that. My father said, "I used to like playing by the water when I was your age. I liked going out on the boats.

That's what made me try to make a living on the sea. It's a tough life. I want something better for you. I want you to go to middle school."

I don't think there was ever a shortage of men like my father in Dongshi, the small town where I grew up. But for more than a decade, the town had slowly developed in the opposite direction, spreading inland as if fleeing from the ocean, which had provided previous generations with great joy and crushed them with suffering. For me, my parents' prohibition made the ocean even more attractive.

On another trip to visit my grandmother, I took my chance. I rushed through the sugarcane. The sound of my mother in sullen pursuit drove me to race ahead even quicker. I ran and jumped into the water. I was swallowed up by the ocean. I sank into the briny embrace. When I looked up, I could see the sunlight filtering down through the water in bright, jagged shards. I closed my eyes, and when I opened them again, I was in a hospital bed.

You can't hide the ocean. My parents tried anyway. They had their own pain, and they wanted to shelter me, out of love. When I heard the ocean crashing in the distance, I always assumed it was just the wind. When I smelled the salt air blowing in from the coast, I always assumed it was coming from the fertilizer plant. But the ocean rose and fell without me, and it kept shining, and it kept calling to me. Because the ocean had been hidden from me, when I finally had the chance to experience it, I took in every detail; I became fanatically devoted to the sea.

After I almost drowned, my father suddenly decided to take me out on a boat. It's a frightening memory. When we got out on the water, I was seasick and kept throwing up until I was too tired even to cry. I begged my father to take me back to shore. After that time, I lost my habit of charging wildly up to the ocean. That's not to say I was afraid of the ocean, but I knew how to appreciate it. I like sitting beside the water, feeling the breeze on my cheek, losing myself in the vast azure blue—even if you're alone, you never feel lonely at that moment looking out on the water. When I was a bit older, I liked going out on my motorcycle and riding up the coast.

You can't hide the ocean, and you can't put a fence around it. The best way is to let people find their own way to appreciate it. Every stretch of sea is a different scene with its own dangers. Life is the same; desire is the same. I used to think I could control each element of my life and live by my own particular logic, to the point where I thought my self-deception was powerful enough to hide things from myself. I thought that was the best way to live. But life is like the ocean: it rises and falls no matter what.

I always wanted to live authentically and honestly; I wanted to be able to accept—perhaps even appreciate— the ups and downs of life. I wanted to be able to live with all shades of emotion and to appreciate human beauty and ugliness in any form. I hoped to take in all of the scenery I saw along the way and express it sensitively in my writing.

I'm determined to find the perfect distance and the best way to appreciate those stretches of sea.

# 11

# A Thousand Identical Cities

Sometime around 1998, my father took it into his head to sell our house in the village and buy a place in Xiamen. The old stone house was a couple thousand square feet, and he was planning to buy a five- or six-hundred-square-foot apartment in the city. He had watched too many Taiwanese TV dramas. Those shows all took place in the city. When he compared life in our small town to life in a big city, he always found suburban life lacking. I recall that it was a particularly rainy spring when he got the idea. When it's hot and muggy like that, you can start to have strange ideas. A feeling of discontentment had spread through the family.

Eventually, my father decided to go to Xiamen to make more serious inquiries, and I was brought along with him. He said it would give me a chance to see life in the big city. Back then, almost everyone from our town got carsick. We didn't have many cars, so we never got used to riding in them. For me, the trigger was the smell of exhaust. As soon as I got on the bus headed for Xiamen, I was hit with a wave of nausea. I jumped out to vomit and looked up to see a parade of cars, each with a tailpipe belching exhaust in my direction. My father wasn't afraid of anything. He had been a sailor. He told me I'd get used to it eventually.

When I got to the city, my sensitive nose seemed unable to find any corner of the city that didn't reek of car exhaust. Packed into a city bus, staring out at the grassy boulevards that lined the road and up at the tall buildings, I tried to work up some enthusiasm for what I was seeing, but nothing in the city seemed particularly interesting. My father did his best to pique my interest. He pointed up at a tall building and said, "How many floors you think that one's got?" I told him I wasn't interested in counting. He said, "You see the way they pave the roads here? That's all brick!" I told him I'd seen streets like that on TV. He asked, "Did you see the streetlights at that last intersection?" I told him that I'd read about things like that before. I simply wasn't interested. I already knew what a big city looked like. A muddy pond in my own backyard held more mystery for me than any corner of Xiamen.

We called on one of my cousins who lived there. He was my cousin, but he was closer in age to my father. He already had a son who was six or so years younger than me. When they saw that I was bored, the boy was charged with taking me out for a walk. I thought I might finally see something interesting, but it was another invitation to count the floors of high-rises and inspect the materials used to pave the streets. The city seemed to be a place of countless rules:

you can't throw garbage all over the place, you have to line up to get on the bus, you have to cross at a crosswalk. . . . I was just a kid, so to me it seemed like a wretched place to grow up. When I saw all that concrete stretching away to the horizon, I felt sad. There weren't any interesting creatures lurking or strange flowers in the scenery. There were no muddy ponds with tadpoles and colorful little fish. There were no places to dig in the dirt.

I'm writing this from Beijing, where the air is so bad it has numbed any sensitivity my nose once had, and I wouldn't be able to appreciate fresh air if I got it. I have been thinking about what it meant to grow up in a place like my hometown. There's a simplicity to people who grow up outside the big city, and with that comes sincerity. I consider Xiamen to be one of the most beautiful cities in China, but I was happy that my father finally decided not to move. I remember talking to Ling Hulei, the creative director at *New Weekly*, about our childhoods. He was from a small town outside Zhanjiang in Guangdong, and I was from a small town outside Quanzhou. By his estimation, we were not outliers. He had noticed the preponderance of suburban and rural young people working in literature and journalism. He put the figure at around 80 percent. Ling Hulei called it "the village laying siege to the city." When he asked me what I thought the reason was, I told him it was because people who grow up in a small town tend to be simple and honest folks.

There are deeper reasons than that basic explanation,

though. People from a small town usually first leave the small town for the nearest city, usually the county capital, and then move on up the ladder until they arrive at a first-tier city. As they make that climb, they get a clear understanding of each level. When they arrive at the next stage, they can look back at where they have come from and have a better understanding of that place and fully assimilate what they might have learned there. On a journey like that, you gain an understanding of your place in things. And on top of all that, kids from small towns just have better stories to tell than city kids.

Again, I don't want it to seem like I am singling out Xiamen. Of all the cities I have been to in China, I would say that Xiamen is one of my favorites, right up there with Kunming. My problem is with cities in general. Most cities in China, and that includes Xiamen, are built according to a simple idea: observe what cities outside China have done and how they organize their citizens, and then copy that model. Modern Chinese cities are not born, nor are they cultivated in an organic way. Everything in a Chinese city is planned. Earlier periods of history were more chaotic, so Chinese cities are built and governed with a strong sense of order controlling how and where people can do certain activities. The people who grow up in that kind of environment have a two-way switch: they can either maintain and support that order or work against it—but they don't often develop any sort of secondary way of looking at the world.

Life needs some turbidity; that goes for the muddy pond

and for our own upbringing. If you compare the water in a muddy pond and the water in a fountain, the water in the pond will always be teeming with life, while the water in the fountain is virtually sterile. A child can spend an entire afternoon watching the countless varieties of life that exist in a muddy pond. A child in the city cannot spend more than a few moments contemplating an urban landscape that has been carefully arranged and planned down to the last detail.

"A thousand identical cities" is a phrase that's become popular with foreign architects to describe the Chinese urban environment. Every single city can be analyzed by standards that are very familiar to those architects, even if they are from outside China. They can see how and why each aspect of the city was planned, but what's missing is any natural, intertwined evolution of people and place. Chinese cities have been deprived of their essence.

In the same way that I prefer Quanzhou to Xiamen, I have always liked Beijing better than Shanghai. The way I see it, Beijing isn't a city at all, but rather the world's largest village. My home in Beijing is close to the bustling hub of Wangfujing, but it is situated down a small *hutong*, one of the narrow alleys that once made up most of the cityscape. I'm still fascinated by my neighborhood in Beijing, where every turn on my walk home from the main road reveals something. Passing a courtyard home converted into a teahouse, I might be lucky enough to hear an old man warming up his voice with local opera, or I might catch a game of chess going on in a corner watched over by a local auntie eating her lunch. Beijing is still capable of offering up pleasant surprises hidden away in its many corners. Beijing is a city with countless layers. It contains multitudes. Shanghai is the complete opposite: an advanced metropolis where if you have seen one part of it, you've seen it all—it all looks the same.

You can make a similar comparison between Quanzhou and Xiamen. I always say that Xiamen is like Quanzhou with a facelift. Quanzhou is a place where the flow of traffic and pedestrians has not yet been tamed, where there are still rough, old buildings, and the nastiest local habits haven't yet been civilized. I like taking in the scenery from the road that goes around the island out in the bay, but it has never really moved me. It could never touch me as deeply as the way the city looks around the festival to mark the Buddha's birthday, when every doorway is hung with offerings, the air is perfumed with incense, everyone is praying for peace, and I hear down a stone alley the sound of someone singing a slow, sad Nanyin ballad.

# 12

# The Question We All Must Answer Eventually

The night before I left Beijing, the weather turned cold. By nine o'clock, the streets were already quiet. I got my mother settled in a hotel in Wudaokou, then took a taxi halfway across Beijing to Li Daren's place in Nancheng. During the whole drive, the wind was howling.

I know I'm making it sound a bit bleak, but that's how I felt at the time. I couldn't say for sure why. I also wasn't sure why I had such an urge to see Li Daren and his daughter, Kiki.

Li Daren's father was in his thirties when the son he was so proud of was born, and by coincidence, Kiki had come along at right around the same point in Li Daren's life. As Li Daren told me about his own father, he hugged Kiki to himself, her small frame resting on his shoulder. Watching Li Daren shower the child with love and kisses, I was moved by his fatherly tenderness.

A year before, when my father passed away, Li Daren

told me that he believed your father's blood flows into your body. I believed that, too.

It was a wonderful coincidence. That's what a relationship between two people always is. A friendship always happens by chance, but it also seems inevitable. Our friends play their own roles in our lives, and they also transform us, molding us into the people we will become. There is a certain logic by which each person leads his or her life, and if I had never met Li Daren, my own individual logic would be completely different.

Li Daren was a direct and passionate man. He was very particular about journalism and people. He had a knack for spotting logical fallacies in his interlocutors; he would never give you the opportunity to cover up those flaws, either. And he wasn't shy about pointing out when someone was being evasive, hesitant, or simply unclear.

Each time I talked to him, I ended up with my feelings hurt. I was often frustrated when he uncovered exactly the thing I was unwilling to say. Sometimes it was a case of not even understanding exactly how I felt, then having Li Daren perfectly sum it up with absolute accuracy. I knew Li Daren only had the best intentions, but after I talked to him, I couldn't help feeling a bit disappointed in how it had gone.

He did the same thing to me on the night I went to see him before I left Beijing. The reason I am writing about that night in particular is because it changed my life.

He asked me, as he always did, "How've you been? Things going okay? Talk to me."

I told him about the time after my father died, how I had spent a few months back home and why I had decided to quit my job to be with him, about my old hometown, motorcycle rides with no destination in mind. I told him how bored I was and how I had lost all interest in my work. And I told him how worried I was about the state I had found myself in.

Li Daren had a habit of chuckling before he spoke. He said, "But that's just an excuse. You know your father's death isn't at the root of all this. That's just your way of avoiding a question you don't want to answer."

At the time, I believed that everything could be explained by my father's stroke eight years prior. Everything revolved around my father's illness, the responsibility I felt toward my family, and the career I had planned to help me provide for them. In my mind, there was a very simple explanation for what I had become. When I was stricken with anxiety about writing a bestseller or becoming a famous author, the reason was that I hoped to be able to shoulder the financial burden of my father's illness. With my father's passing, I felt like I had lost what had once been the focus of my life. I thought my indecisiveness and worry were natural.

So when Li Daren told me I was using all that to avoid facing something, I was angry. He explained himself, though: "The question is, how do you want to live your life? You still don't have the courage to answer."

He didn't explain himself further, but I thought I understood what he wanted to say. I didn't know how I wanted to live my life, so I had replaced any real consideration of the question with a narrow, utilitarian logic that relied on a ready-made excuse. I didn't have any goals beyond getting as rich as possible and as famous as possible, and I had covered up even that with pretty words like "dreams" and "responsibilities."

Now that some time has gone by, I appreciate Li Daren's care and attention. I treasure his words.

I don't think I am in the minority in getting by without really knowing how to live my life. People like me reach for the easiest excuses—our dreams and our responsibilities—to avoid answering that key question.

Since leaving Beijing and returning to Fujian, I have been thinking about the person I was for the eight years after my father's stroke. I had passed the juncture where I should have begun to consider how to define myself, to decide how I was going to live and what goals I should work toward, but I had used my family's misfortune as an excuse not to face those questions.

I threw myself into my work, keeping myself constantly under pressure so that I would never have any free time. I didn't want to have to figure out how to fill that free time, and I didn't want to ever have time to ponder how I should live my life, what I really thought was valuable, and what I really enjoyed.

I was fundamentally unwilling to pass judgment on my own life. I also couldn't manage to take control over it. I was always running away, hiding behind what I described as my responsibility to my family. I chased after the news and called it chasing my dream. Everything in my life moved with the rhythm of my job, so I became fragile, capable of being unsettled and frightened at the slightest turbulence.

That night, Li Daren's final words to me were "Think hard about your life. Figure out how to actually enjoy it." I thought I understood what he wanted to say. Life isn't simple; it comes with hardships. It's more complicated than simply staying true to what you call your ideals, and the meaning of living an authentic life is up to us to decide.

Perhaps life is like a questionnaire. When you refuse to answer a question, you can't go on to the next question, and that unanswered query continues to follow you around.

When I left Li Daren's house that night, it was already eleven o'clock. From that moment on, I felt an unprecedented comfort and relaxation. Before that, I had been avoiding my friends. I couldn't face myself, so there was no way I could face them.

I was suddenly anxious to get in touch with my friend Chenggang, whose calls I had been avoiding. He was the deputy director of the newspaper in my hometown. He was a workaholic who loved talking to me about journalism and about life. He was committed to his ideals. After my father died, he had often called to cheer me up.

Sometimes life is like a bad soap opera. The morning after I talked to Li Daren, I got a call from Yifa telling me that Chenggang had died. He was just over thirty and had been taken out by a heart attack. For a man so committed to his ideals, it seemed an appropriate way for him to go.

Forgive me, Chenggang, my brother, my teacher, my intimate friend. The whole way back home to see you off, I was blaming you—for not answering the question either and for leaving behind a wife and daughter, and leaving friends like me with infinite regrets over your short life. I wish I could have talked to you about how to enjoy your life, to tell you that we should never have filled our heads with false dreams. I wish I could have talked to you about what we should cherish most in this life and what we should have realized was really valuable.

Forgive me, Father, for throwing myself into my work after you got sick. I thought that was how I could make you happy. But when I saw the photo you kept of me, the only one I had given you, worn pale by the stroking of your fingers, I knew I had deprived you of what only I could give you, what was most valuable to you then.

I wrote this for my father, and for my good friend Wang Chenggang.

# 13

# Homecoming

I still felt the familiar comfort: I knew every stone, and every stone knew me. I knew every corner of the neighborhood and how the years had collected there, transforming them, and every corner of the neighborhood had also looked back, watching time change me.

I returned to my hometown to convalesce, but as I lay on my sickbed, it was my power of recollection that seemed to have recovered. Thinking back over everything that had happened in the past several years, I concluded that the only thing I could take pride in was choosing my father's burial plot.

As far as cemeteries go, it was a high-end neighborhood, and my mother wasn't happy with the price. It was a display of vanity, but I cherished my ability to finally do something for my father, to whom I had never been able to give a better life.

After my father passed, his urn had been placed in a columbarium near his old school. It was my mother's idea, since she volunteered at a nearby temple, and it was convenient for her to stop by on her way there and wish her husband a good morning. She had also taken his waistline into consideration. "He's getting fat," she told me, "so I thought he might appreciate having the sports field at the school right there, since he used to like to exercise."

In my hometown, there was a nearly universal belief that the gods were watching and the spirits of the departed were always lurking. Our world and the netherworld were separated by only a thin membrane. Everyone knew that spirits lived much like we did, just on the other side of the barrier between worlds. Spirits got hungry, sometimes they ate too much, and sometimes they started to pack on the pounds. Spirits could be happy or sad or bored or sick. . . . My father went on living much as he always had, still in our hometown. On the anniversary of his passing, she burned agarwood incense in front of the memorial tablet on the altar and asked, "How was the marinated duck?" Every now and then, someone in the family would catch some sign of his presence, and when they told my mother, she would stop by to read sutras for him. "You need to read these," she would tell him sternly, "or you'll never get into the Western Paradise."

That went on for a few years, until Second Uncle unexpectedly passed away. His son, who had done well in business, wanted to lay his father to rest somewhere nice.

He toured the cemeteries of the area by car, weighing up the advantages and disadvantages of each. He eventually settled on the Old Plum Mound Garden, which had been built with money from a Taiwanese businessman.

The price was steep, but my uncle was insistent. He wanted the two brothers to be together again. "They were so close," he said. "Why separate them now?"

The way he imagined it, the two brothers would hang out like they always had, drinking and telling stories, running off somewhere to catch a show. . . . Their two younger brothers—Third Uncle and Fourth Uncle—were in full agreement; the cousins were unanimous. My mother, though, was hesitant. She refused to explain exactly why she was holding back, and finally, one of the aunts was dispatched to ask her directly. "It's too expensive," she said, "and anyway, it's too far away. You know I get carsick. It'll be impossible for me to get out there. . . ." She went on in that vein for a while.

When all other efforts had been exhausted, I was recruited to press my mother to make a decision. She decided it would be my responsibility to make the final call. Since my father had his stroke when I was in my second year of high school, she had given me the role of head of the family, and it was often my place to pass final judgment on things like this.

I was in Guangzhou during that period, and I rushed back home to see the cemetery my uncle had selected. I was haunted by a need to pay my father back. I hadn't cried when my father passed. I was furious at myself, because I had lost my chance to do anything for him. I owed him so much, and I feared the debt would go forever unpaid. The cemetery plot was one way I could pay him back. Perhaps my mother still had misgivings, but she had to accept my decision.

The day my father was to be moved from his school-adjacent resting place to the upscale cemetery, my mother spent the whole day crying. She wouldn't tell anybody the reason, and she resisted any efforts to cheer her up. The sulking was contagious, and I eventually took her aside to ask her what the problem was. She looked like a child speaking through sobs: "I just can't stop thinking there's no way I can see him every day now."

On the day my father was to be moved to his new resting place, I was in charge of carrying his heavy stone urn. As I struggled to make my way toward the new plot, lugging the urn, one of my cousins joked to my father, "You must be eating good over there, put on some pounds, huh? This scrawny little son of yours can't even carry you now."

The weight of the urn became even more of an issue when it was time to lower it into the tomb. I didn't think I had the strength to place it just right without reaching down inside. According to what the feng shui master of the place had told me, though, it was taboo for a living soul to enter the tomb, and that included the shadow of a person.

We finally figured out a way to get the ashes into the

tomb with me lying flat on my stomach and the cousins placing the urn into my hands so that I could put it in place.

Lying flat on that patch of land into which my father would soon be placed, I felt as close to it as I would with my cheek pressed to the chest of a loved one. I placed the urn in the ground as gently as I could, and everyone cheered. I couldn't stop myself from discreetly shedding a few unexpected tears. I was sure my father would be happy with the choice I had made. I wasn't sure why, but I was sure. I had laid myself down on that soil and felt the warmth and comfort of it.

When I woke up the next morning, my mother told me about a dream she had the night before. My father had said to her, "Blackie bought me a new house. It's very nice." She smiled at me then, but she spent most of the next several days in a dark mood because she was no longer able to visit him daily.

Frankly, I still had some regrets over moving my father. The plot at the cemetery was about a hundred square feet, but it would never live up to the massive tombs my favorite ancestors had been buried in.

Those tombs were over four hundred square feet. They had a burial mound in the center, where the actual remains of the deceased were interred, a memorial stone and altar in front of that for making offerings, and then a narrow, raised platform running in a horseshoe shape around the back and sides.

When family members got together to clean the tomb and offer sacrifices, they lit candles and burned incense on the altar, and stuck colored paper to the platform.

The last time I had been out to the tombs for Qingming, the festival of tidying up the graves of ancestors, it was a humid day with a bit of wind. I remember sweating while putting up the colored paper and feeling the moist breeze running over my skin.

I have always liked Qingming. It's a moment for the family to come together to tend to the final resting places of shared ancestors. The scene at Qingming was never static: each year, the old people had grown older, and there were always new arrivals into the family. The older family members you work alongside on Qingming will one day make their way to the other side, and you will come together again—but one of you will be under the earth and the other above it. The young people who share the day with you will one day be the ones to sweep your tomb. The tradition gives me a sense of steadfastness in the world, so that I no longer fear life or death.

I had returned home to recuperate, but since it was Qingming, I followed everyone out to clean the graves of my father and uncle, then in the afternoon I insisted on going along with the rest of the family up the mountain path to the tombs that housed my grandmother, my grandfather, my great-grandmother and great-grandfather, and so on up the family tree. . . . The mountainside was bright with strips of colored paper, the sound of family members paying their respects, and the pop of firecrackers. The smell of black powder mixing with the scent of the earth after the rain—for me, that was the smell of Qingming. It was a smell I knew from a time when I was one of the youngest, while on those later visits, I was surrounded by young people who addressed me as uncle even though they were nearly as tall as I was, and who even wanted to ask me about politics.

At the graves of my grandfather and grandmother, the family, tied together by blood, continued the tradition. They sat together on the platform around the mounds, as if sitting on the laps of the venerable deceased.

At that moment, I felt like a growth ring in a split log, pressed peacefully between countless other concentric circles.

I believed in spirits; I believed that my father visited my mother in her dream. When I lay down on the earth into which my father was about to be placed, I felt a deep connection, and it was just like my father, I thought, to describe his resting place as his home. A home is not simply a structure that gives one shelter but a place you are linked to by blood and soil.

After I left my hometown and went far away, whenever I encountered setbacks or felt like my resolve was weakening, my first urge was to rush home, even though the trip was often inconvenient.

My mother used to tell me, speaking our local Minnan language, "If you don't come back for the New Year, you might as well not have a home; if you don't sweep the tombs on Qingming, you might as well not have ancestors." What my mother had said was part of the reason I went back home for the festival, but there was something beyond that, too, something gnawing at me that I wasn't sure what to do about.

I had accrued plenty of airline miles on business trips and ashen-faced flights home, and I traded them in for a ride in glorious business class. When I told my mother on the phone about cashing in my miles earned rushing around the country for a ride home in luxurious and expensive comfort, I realized it was something of a metaphor for my life.

The flight home was full of people just like me, all returning to the southern coast of Fujian from the big city. Everyone in business class, carrying gifts and offerings for the festival, was speaking my mother tongue. "I've got to get out to my uncle's grave this time," I overheard one man saying. "I remember the way he used to put me on his knee when I was a boy and feed me guava." "It's too bad you never got to meet your grandmother," another woman said. "She used to always save the best morsels for me. . . ." I realized that I was living a life nearly identical to many other Minnan people and overseas Chinese. We ran around until we were ready to drop dead, just so we could return home with dignity.

That Qingming afternoon, during a lull in the ceremonies, my mother started teasing me about my home-sickness. She told a story. During university, when I was doing whatever it took to help my family scrape by, one of my many part-time jobs was tutoring students at an exam prep school, and one day I almost collapsed from over-work. A few people got together to drag me to the hospital, but I was delirious from fever and kept refusing. Instead of seeing a doctor, I told them, slipping in and out of con-sciousness, yelling hysterically through tears, "I want to go home, I want to go home."

Why did I want to go home? After the fever went down, I opened my eyes and found myself in my own bed. My mother told me that nobody could talk me into going to the hospital, so they put me in a taxi and sent me home. "What is it about home?" my mother said, teasing me. "Why did you want to come home?" I tried to come up with an an-swer to her questions, but I was left speechless. I blushed.


What is it about home?

I had gone through so much while I was away, the trip home was long and arduous, and in the days after I returned to my hometown, I pondered what had lured me back. When I looked at things without emotion, my hometown was dull. The neighborhood was chaotic, full of hideous buildings, most of them with rough stone foun-dations and upper walls of reinforced concrete. Even the homes built of red brick by the overseas Chinese were set side-by-side with huts made of rammed earth and shacks where migrant workers kept flocks of ducks on the roof.

I particularly liked the few stone alleys that remained. When it rained, they became treacherous, but strolling there, I still felt the romance of them—until I came across a new artery full of concrete. There were temples everywhere in those alleys, and the smell of agarwood incense still puffed out onto the street—until the dust and smells of a construction site overpowered them.

I couldn't help but ask myself, *Why am I still dependent on this place?*

The afternoon of Qingming, I returned to the neighborhood alone and walked through the cityscape I knew so well. I took an umbrella and walked over to my old elementary school. With all the kids off for the festival, it felt deserted. I cut through the noisy wet market, where the same middle-aged woman was still plying her trade at the marinated meat stall, cutting each item with laser precision. I paused in front of the old hunchback who sells sea worm jelly out of a rusty metal box. I decided to order a few pieces, watched as he dressed the balls of gelatin with garnishes, then stood off to the side and ate. . . . When I got home, I decided to take my motorcycle out, without telling my mother where I was going. I rode out to the coast and walked around for a while. After returning from the coast, I felt a bit light-headed, but there was a sense of relief, too, to be back at home.

I still felt the familiar comfort. I knew every stone, and

every stone knew me. I knew every corner of the neighborhood and how the years had collected there, transforming them, and every corner of the neighborhood had also looked back, watching time change me.

When I got home, I went up to the fourth floor of the house and looked out over the town. With the rain misting down, the flagstone roads looked even more lush, and the red brick houses seemed to glow. Down in the mess of construction and ramshackle half-renovated homes below, through the smoke from the industrial district, an old woman with flowers in her hair came up the road carrying a basket back from the wet market, followed by a convoy of fishermen back from the coast and a voice echoing from down some lane, singing a tune in the Minnan language. . . . I felt deep down that those were the ingredients of my soul. Maybe it's not quite right to say that my heart contains this landscape, but this landscape is what formed me.


After a few days of indulgence, I decided it was time to start my convalescence in earnest. I lay in my bed with the seemingly endless rain falling outside. I felt like a kid again, lazily soaking up the smell of wet earth as I stretched out in my bed. The moisture and warmth of the place was so familiar and comfortable, it felt like the embrace of a loved one. I felt incredible comfort wash over me. I thought of my father entombed in the earth and decided that he must feel the same as I felt.

I have liked the smell of the earth since I was young. I was never afraid of death, since it would simply mean returning home, back to the soil of my native place. On the contrary, it was living that was a problem. Babies crawl, then they learn to stand up because they want to break free from the earth. After they stand, they keep climbing, pushing forward, driven by desire, ideals, ambition. But our feet are forever bound to the soil. Comparing life and death, it is life that makes more demands upon us. Perhaps living too intensely represents a kind of willfulness, but it's not always the way of life we should pursue.

That afternoon, smelling the thick, fresh scent of the earth, I fell into a deep sleep.

In my dream, I was a child again, wandering away from home. I was walking barefoot down one of the stone alleys. I knew the people in the alley, and I knew the stones. The people and the stones asked me where I was going. I told them I was going to take a look, just a look. I started to run down the alley, racing wildly past the stones and the people, who both called out to me with warnings. I slowly realized that my headfirst rush had carried me to an unfamiliar place. I didn't recognize the feeling of the place. I didn't recognize the stones. The red bricks were gone. I felt a sudden panic, as if I were plunging into a dark cavern. It felt as if the ground had dropped out below me. I began to cry, but my curiosity kept me sharp, forcing me to take in the unfamiliar scenery.

It was a beautiful place. There was a beach I had never seen before, whose name I did not know. There were a few big boats floating out on the water, and a flock of seabirds skimmed the surface of the water. I could have spent the rest of my afternoon there—but it wasn't home. I couldn't hold back my fear. Why was it so windy? Why was the sand so dry? Where were the stones I knew? I glanced back and saw that the stone alley was waiting for me not far away.

I ran for the alley as if I were being chased. I was running and crying, running and laughing, all at the same time, and I kept going until I was at my own front door. I pounded my fists on the door, and my mother opened. She knew nothing of my narrow escape, but she saw my pale face covered in tears. She didn't ask what was wrong; she didn't scold me for wandering away. She opened the door wider and said, "What are you doing? Why don't you come inside?"

I used the last ounce of energy in my legs to drag myself into the house. The smell of the stove, moist wood, and dog embraced me. In that moment, I knew I was home. I lay down on the dirty floor. And when I woke up from the dream, I started to cry. Perhaps, I thought, I had never left my hometown at all, but merely strayed for a while, seen the beauty of a new place, and scared myself. I had returned home, and I knew that I could always come back. I would always find the narrow alley that led me back to where I belonged.

# 14

# Where Is This Train Going?

I must have passed by at least once
The river where you bathed
Your childhood at age six
Floats on the surface of the water
I looked up
Saw a massive
Tangerine
Hanging above me
I know
This is childhood's
Every dusk

—"Every Travel Story"

I wrote that poem on the train to Nanping sometime in my first year of high school. The trip had been a reward for myself, and it was the first time I'd taken the train alone.

Because southern Fujian used to be considered a maritime front line, it never had many train lines built, and this route into the mountains was one of the few.

I had boarded the train at the coast and was being carried into a lush mountain landscape. Light and shadow slipped by the window like a stream. I watched houses set along the tracks approaching at great speed, then being pulled into the distance just as quickly. In a ruined courtyard, I saw an old woman cradling her crying granddaughter, then there was a man sitting on a block outside a gate puffing on a cigarette, and then there was a young girl, book bag slung over her back, looking intently at the closed door of a house, as if hesitating to go inside—and each person slipped away as the train pulled me onward.

I started to try to imagine the lives of these people with whom the train put me into brief contact as I passed, but they just kept coming, until finally the sun began to set, and the train pulled me far from the town and into the country, where there were only occasional pinpoints of light in the hazy mountain scenery. The orange glow of the sunset fluttered like satin, shifting over the landscape as if being rustled by the hands of a playful child.

I was ambushed by unexpected emotion. What was happening out there, where those faint lights shone? What had made the old woman take the child into her arms? What was the man thinking about as he sat smoking beside the gate? Why was the girl hesitating to open the door?

The pleasure of travel is that everything slips by so

quickly. The traveler treads lightly and happily. But there is a dark side to this as well: since everything slips by so quickly, it never becomes anything more than scenery.

That trip I took in my first year of high school suddenly came to mind one day while visiting my old university. A former professor had invited me back to speak to new students. "What We See Along the Way" was the topic he suggested for the talk. Before the speech began, sitting in my former seat in a classroom where I had attended many lectures, memories came flooding back to me.

Whatever you are going through, it is often the length of time you experience it, as much as the experience itself, that makes it brutal.

Nine years earlier, sitting in that same classroom, my mind was in a different place, occupied with thoughts of my father, half his body paralyzed by a stroke, my family plunged into a horrible predicament from which there seemed no way out. Thinking back, I felt as if I was seeing another person who happened to share my name. What was Cai Chongda thinking? He wanted to figure out how to make enough money to send his father to get treatment in the United States. He would give up simple luxuries if it meant he could save up enough to send Nana on a trip. Cai Chongda was ready to risk it all. He wanted to be famous. He wanted to make his old boss, Wang Chenggang, proud of him. Cai Chongda had promised him he would someday write a book and carry a message to the children of the patients at Fujian Second People's Hospital, tell them that there was still hope, that they should never give up. . . .

The Cai Chongda who returned to the classroom that day had lost his drive and idealism. His father was gone, Nana was gone, and Chenggang was gone. The new Cai Chongda had lost touch with the real world and seemed instead to float above it. The only way he could keep contact with solid ground was to throw himself into his work.

For the past several years, I have lived in the gap between worlds. When it came to my life, I was never willing to take any real steps forward. In my work as a journalist I played the role of the dispassionate recorder of events, a casual observer of things. I could press myself into the crowd and get swept up in their rage or joy, but I would always harden my heart and walk away from it all.

I started to think of myself as a constant traveler. Just like on that first train trip I took into the mountains, I let people approach, sometimes shared a moment, and then roared past. I tried to remind myself that it wasn't any good to be caught up in something emotionally, because life, like a train, keeps rolling. There is no way to freeze a moment in time. Eventually, I became accustomed to my role. I learned to be indifferent. I thought of myself as a traveler even when I appeared settled.

The invitation to speak at the university had come, completely by coincidence, as I happened to be headed back to my hometown to apply for travel documents for Hong

Kong and Macao. The memories that day in the classroom were a long-delayed collision with reality, delivered like a hammer blow to the head.

When I got back to my hometown, I went for a tour on my motorcycle. I saw that the tavern my father opened years ago had been turned into a warehouse. The gas station had been knocked down, and there were plans to put a park on top of it. Nana's old house had been carved up into lodgings for migrant workers, and the rose bush I loved so much had withered away to a few twisted branches. When I went to Quanzhou to visit the newspaper office where I had once worked with Chenggang, Director Zhang, who had been promoted following Chenggang's passing, showed me an official document announcing that the newspaper office would be closed at the end of next year.

Director Zhang invited me out for a couple of drinks, but I made an excuse and a hasty exit. As soon as I got outside, I broke down in tears. I was afraid that if he brought up Chenggang's name and how the poor man had worked himself to death, neither of us would be able to keep our composure.

Time is cruel. My father might have been a weak man, but he was a good man, and he disappeared without a trace. Chenggang, whom I considered to be my brother, had thrown himself into his work, fighting his way through life, just to sparkle for an instant and then be extinguished. And Nana, whom I loved so much, who seemed as un-moving as a boulder, had been wiped away, too. That is the way life is: people go through life and then are swept away, disappearing without much trace that they ever lived, often without even a place to visit to evoke their memory.

And for me, living my life as I was still aboard that train, all I could do was shout myself hoarse—and I knew that would be useless. There was no way to smash the glass and call out to the people I loved, no way to stop the train and kiss them or take them in an embrace, no way I could insist on staying with them. . . . Any attempt to slow the onward rush of life would prove useless.

I realized one day that I could no longer accept living that way. I didn't want to be a traveler constantly passing through, as if on the run from something. Human life might be a journey, but it takes a certain mindset and certain abilities for a person to appreciate the scenery seen during a life spent constantly on the road. I didn't want to float through life, my feet never planted anywhere for long. I wanted to settle down somewhere, to take root, to sprout, to grow, and to provide shelter for my loved ones.

To those I love and those who love me, I ask for your understanding. Even if it proves futile, I will do everything I can to slow down the onward rush of time. I will carve your memory into my bones, so that even if your physical body is swept away, I carry with me your name and your memory. That is the only way I can resist the passage of time.

I have never understood why the train of life has to rush by at the speed it does, forking off down countless

detours. Like a child throwing a tantrum, I refuse to accept
it. Where are we going, and why do we have to get there
so quickly? I know it's not only me who can't accept it. I
might be one of those who raise a voice in complaint, but
I know that even those who remain silent are dissatisfied.
Maturity can't help you accept it, either; maturity only
helps you gain the ability to deceive yourself. I remember
that when I got back from that first train trip I wrote another short poem, called "The World":

This is not a big world
There is nowhere I need to be
I could stay here
Watching you
Until everything grows old

It was a fairly juvenile piece of poetry, but I haven't
matured much beyond when I wrote it. I'm just as childish.
The idea expressed in the poem encapsulates my childish
resistance to the passage of time: I want to halt the onward
rush and hold on to what I treasure most, but I continu-
ally find myself powerless. I don't want to lose that feeling,
even if it is naive. Even if I am rushing forward, I want to
try to travel alongside the ones I love as long as I can; even
if I am rushing forward, I hope we can become the beautiful scenery of each other's lives—that is all I am capable of.
    I wrote this for a friend of mine, putting into writing
many things that had been on my mind. I wanted to thank

him. Even if time and fate are cruel, I wanted to thank them, too, for what they have shown me. Everything inevitably has a dark side and a bright side. If you want to float through life, treading as lightly as possible, you must learn to compromise. My friend is the one who first wrote, "Maturity can't help us accept things; maturity only helps us gain an ability to deceive ourselves and others." Is there any way to get through life without developing that sort of pessimism?

# Afterword

O n my thirtieth birthday, I happened to be in London. The planned itinerary had me at the British Museum.

The museum has rotating galleries in the main spaces, and the day I went, there was one called *Living and Dying*. Part of the gallery was an installation called *Cradle to Grave* showing the medical history of individuals represented by various pharmaceuticals and medical equipment arranged in columns on a long table. At the bottom of each column were photographs of the deceased at his happiest and saddest moments, and then in the final moments of his life.

Looking at those faces, I suddenly thought of my father and the eight years of illness that preceded his passing. It occurred to me that my father had just turned thirty, too, when I came into his life.

I walked up and down the installation, studying each photograph, contemplating each life, and I couldn't stop thinking about my father. He must have been a lot like me when he turned thirty, freshly passed from ignorance to enlightenment, scoured of all naïveté, life beginning to crimp wrinkles into his cheeks, and coming face-to-face with reality. Had he found a way to reconcile his desires with that reality? Did he comprehend the new life that was rushing his way? However he felt, whatever he thought, his eventual fate was lurking even then, waiting to take him captive. . . .

It was then that I realized I had never truly known my father, even if we were the most important part of each other's life. Strictly speaking, I only knew my father's life and his story in his role as my father. Beyond that, though, I had never really seen him; I had never understood him except as my father.

The realization made me extremely sad.

I often tell my friends that the greatest kindness you can do someone is to try to understand them. When you sit down with people, look them in the eyes, and listen to them speak, you see all the twists and turns, key moments, and fate that led them to where they are; you can see what carved them into their current state; and when you learn about the way they see the world and how they use that knowledge, you can begin to understand them. When you look at people like that, you are truly seeing them.

I had never truly seen my father, and I had lost my chance. I started to worry that I would repeat that mistake with other people in my life. The awareness of the possibility was a fear planted deep in my heart.

A month after I returned from London, I began to try using memories of my father to construct an essay. I wanted to search for traces of my father, to reach out and touch what I could of him, and to attempt to truly see him. That essay became "Frailty." I thought it was the best possible way to retain some memory of him and bid him farewell, and also to record some of my own fear and anxiety.

Finishing that essay created a sense of urgency in me: I did not want to stop with my father. If I could make an attempt to truly see my father, I thought I should try to see other people in my life, too, and to honor them in the same way. I was going to walk upstream against the rush of time to attempt to preserve something of them. It was also a way for me to understand myself. After all, it is the people in our lives who form us into the person we see in the mirror.

After I came to that decision, writing this book was no longer something I wanted to do but rather something I needed to do. Before embarking on this project, I had seen writing as mostly a matter of technical ability, but now I realize it's about expression and about giving readers a window through which they might truly see other people, their world, and all of the possibilities contained within. Literature completes us.

Once I came to this realization, writing became even more difficult.

I made a living in journalism, but before that, I was a bookish boy with dreams of writing. I went into media work to support myself, but I had a secret goal, too: to improve my skills as a writer in preparation for a return to the literary world. I worked in media for eleven years, turned out 2.6 million characters of copy, and found a place for more complex and wide-ranging writing. I thought I finally had the talent to face the world, to face myself, and to face everyone I cared about, but that turned out not to be the case.

When I started crafting these essays, I realized that writing is like surgery, but I was using the scalpel on myself. When I wrote about other people, I could put their pain into my writing without taking it on myself. But when I began to write this book, each expression of pain recorded by my pen was carved into my own heart. That was what gave authenticity to the writing. I finally understood why most writers' first books are about themselves and their own individual concerns: a writer must dissect himself before he can turn his attention to other people.

A few of the essays in this book felt, while I was writing them, as if they were being sucked from my very bone marrow. These were stories I cared about deeply, and they were precious to me. I knew them so well it was as if they had been carved into my bones. When it came time to write, it was almost like laying a sheet of paper over those carvings and making a rubbing.

While writing "My Mother's House," I finally came to an understanding of my mother's undying but inexpressible love; while writing "Vessel," I understood my nana's legacy; while writing "Friends in High Places," I realized what people do to escape the onslaught of emotion. . . .

And while writing this, I realize how important it is to truly see the people I treasure and to uncover their answers to the questions we all face.

We are lucky that everyone is different. That's what makes our world so rich. And we're also lucky that there are so many commonalities among people. If you make an effort, you can see the things people share. It is in those commonalities that we reflect one another and bring warmth to each other.

I think this is the ultimate meaning of writing, and also the ultimate meaning of reading. I hope that my book can help readers truly see other people and themselves.

This book is dedicated to my father and to Nana, both no longer with us, to my mother, who has been there every step of the way, and to my wife, my sister, and my daughter.

I love you, and I know you love me.

# A Note from the Translator

I have always gone looking in books for expressions of the thoughts and feelings that I am unable or ashamed or frightened to express myself; I have found many in Cai Chongda's *Vessel*. Like any worthwhile memoir, *Vessel* is a testament to how a writer's vulnerability can provoke deep emotion.

I translated many of my favorite sections of *Vessel* in tears. Cai Chongda's writing about his father in particular hit close to home for me. This is a book that I challenge any reader to get through stone-faced. Perhaps part of the emotion, for me, while translating, came from the idea that I would be the conduit—someone, somewhere would be sniffling over the scene of Cai returning to his childhood home and finding the picture of himself that his father had worn white by caressing it with the one hand still left mobile after his stroke. In moments when I was overcome by emotion, I always kept typing, hoping to stay tapped into the emotion of Cai Chongda's bittersweet revelations, hoping that readers of this translation would get to feel them as deeply as I did. For those sections, I hope that I did not violate rules of faithfulness, but I took as a more crucial job the transmission of the jolt of frisson that I believe Cai Chongda intended.

I see this as a very special book. It was a bestseller beyond the borders of the People's Republic of China. Comparisons to American memoirs, like Jeannette Walls's *The Glass Castle* and J. D. Vance's *Hillbilly Elegy*, are not only for the benefit of foreign readers—the same comparisons were made by Chinese readers, who are accustomed to reading memoirs by notable people and business leaders, but not so much naked sentimental and deeply personal accounts of growing up in a small town.

In the context of Chinese literature in translation, *Vessel* feels even more special. More than any other nation's modern literature, Chinese books in translation have been affected by ideology. There seems to be, in Chinese literature in translation, a preference for the epic and didactic; books that might inform the reader about events like the Cultural Revolution or the protests of 1989. *Vessel* is a break from much of what makes it into translation: Cai Chongda's story is not a rags-to-riches tale of fortunes won in the New China, but a more relatable journey from a precarious middle class identity to potentially equally precarious comfort in Beijing in his early twenties.

I think it's a shame that Chinese literature in translation is so often promoted for its didactic utility. This book, like any from a foreign literature, can inform the reader about life in a faraway place, but what makes *Vessel* special is what it might tell us about ourselves.

—Dylan Levi King

Here ends Cai Chongda's
*Vessel.*

The first edition of this book was printed and
bound at LSC Communications in
Harrisonburg, Virginia, July, 2021.

# A Note on the Type

This novel was set in Bembo, a typeface originally cut
by Francesco Griffo in 1495, and revived by Stanley
Morrison in 1929. Named after the Venetian poet
and Cardinal Pietro Bembo (1470–1547), Griffo's
original punch-cut design was a departure from
the popular calligraphic style of the day. It's warm,
human touch would inspire later roman typefaces
like Garamond and Times Roman. Morrison, one of
the twentieth century's most influential typographers,
revived the typeface for typesetting and machine
composition. Bembo is noted for its attractiveness
on the page and high legibility, making it a popular
choice for printed matter.

## HARPERVIA

An imprint dedicated to publishing international voices,
offering readers a chance to encounter other lives and other
points of view via the language of the imagination.